We only need one person to understand.
Will you be the one?

Life brings us down unexpected paths,
but who we meet along the way can
bring much-needed clarity.

When we can finally get to the
understanding that our journey brings
us to exactly where we are supposed to
be and perhaps there were lessons that
needed to be learned, the clarity comes.

I know every bit of pain was necessary,
just as every bit of love was needed.

Together, we are better.
Together, we are stronger.
Together, we can make a difference.

i understand

i understand

Pain, Love, and Healing after Suicide

Vonnie Woodrick

WITHDRAWN

WILLIAM B. EERDMANS PUBLISHING COMPANY
GRAND RAPIDS, MICHIGAN

Wm. B. Eerdmans Publishing Co.
4035 Park East Court SE, Grand Rapids, Michigan 49546
www.eerdmans.com

26 25 24 23 22 21 20   1 2 3 4 5 6 7

ISBN 978-0-8028-7804-5

Library of Congress Cataloging-in-Publication Data

Names: Woodrick, Vonnie, 1964– author.
Title: I understand : pain, love, and healing after suicide / Vonnie
    Woodrick.
Description: Grand Rapids, Michigan : William B. Eerdmans
    Publishing Company, 2020. | Summary: "One woman's pain and
    healing following her husband's death from suicide leads to a
    movement calling for change in the way we think about mental
    illness and suicide"—Provided by publisher.
Identifiers: LCCN 2020016401 | ISBN 9780802878045 (paperback)
Subjects: LCSH: Mental health—Religious aspects—Christianity.
    | Suicide—Religious aspects—Christianity. | Woodrick, Vonnie,
    1964–
Classification: LCC BT732.4 .W58 2020 | DDC 248.8/628—dc23
LC record available at https://lccn.loc.gov/2020016401

CONTENTS

FOREWORD

The journey of understanding our lives, our families, and the reasons we have to go through tragedies and loss is a long one. I have an intimate connection with i understand—the organization and now a book. I was the keynote speaker in 2017 for an i understand event in Michigan. Prior to going there, I didn't think too much about it, as I speak all over the country about mental health, addiction, and the suicide that has been a part of my family for generations. I enjoy sharing my story about my struggles with understanding my legacy because it always teaches me something more about myself. I also share because I feel that we all come from stories of loss or trauma, or something that has been a challenge for us but has gotten us to where we are in our lives currently. I arrived in Michigan three years ago; Vonnie met me at the airport, and we began a two-day journey that would touch my heart.

Vonnie introduced her daughters to me, both beautiful, intelligent, and looking for opportunities to talk with me. Her son too, was dealing with his family history and eager to share that with me. He dealt with his trauma through the books he read and the relationships he made through the authors who had touched his life (he happened to love my grandfather's work, so we had that in common). But it was when I began talking with Maddie, Vonnie's youngest daughter, that I felt a familial connection. You know when that happens . . . you meet someone, a total stranger, who is not strange to you at all. You simply feel a sense of comfort in their presence. I realize now that that is why I tell my story: because once in a while a person like Maddie comes along and my words resonate with her, and then my own life makes sense. It is a gift when you meet someone who sees the world from the same perspective as you do.

Maddie was newly in college then, and, although she was young, her understanding of literature and of my grandfather's writings felt incredibly succinct and familiar to me. While we were speaking, she made special reference to my grandfather Ernest Hemingway's short story "Up in Michigan" (written about a place in which she and my grandfather had both grown up). She asked interesting and pertinent questions about the story and its relevance to the modern world we live in today. It was intriguing. Maddie also read my own book, *Out Came the Sun*, and she seemed to understand it at a cellular level. Like me, she uses nature, mountains, and the outdoors as a way to bring meaning to the thoughts in her head and the past she has overcome. She processes her life through her connection to the wild exactly as I have done for decades. We were/are soul sisters, for lack of a better term. After a somewhat brief exchange, I felt seen by her, and I knew that she felt seen and understood by me. My connection with Maddie and all of Vonnie's family is linked to the whole reason behind the story of i understand. Just like my story of the Hemingway legacy, it is not about the fame of my family or the fact that I am a public figure . . . it is about the power of sharing your story. The impact of storytelling and how it can heal you is important. When we share our journey, whether it is ugly and weak or strong and bittersweet, it takes the sting out of the past. It gives all of us permission to have and share our—not always pretty—journey. Once you tell your story, you can begin to heal.

For herself and her amazing family, Vonnie has taken the time to write down the story of her life and her life's mission to make a difference in the world of mental illness and suicide with her organization, i understand, and in doing so she gives us all reason to step up and be honest about the families we come from. Not all of us have suicide or depression or even mental illness in our lives, but I can almost guarantee that there is some secret story about our past that we allow to define us. This book is an invitation to be brave enough to share our demons with others, so that we can let them go. Whether it is with a close friend, a spouse, or a family member, maybe even in a public forum, wherever one shares one's journey is not pertinent. The important thing is that you write or voice your family secret. In doing so, you begin to release the power that it has on you. When you speak truth to your life, the story it comes from becomes just that . . . a story: a lesson that has colored your past, not a sentence that interrupts your future.

—*Mariel Hemingway*

PREFACE

A person never truly gets "over" a suicide loss. You get through it. Day by day. Sometimes moment by moment.

—Holly Kohler

After losing my husband, Rob, to suicide, I was devastated, confused, and heartbroken. No life experience could have prepared me for suicide's claim on my husband. I was left to wonder, "What happened?" I thought suicide was something that happened to other people, other families. Only crazy people die by suicide, right? Yet my husband wasn't crazy; he was kind, gentle, and loving. How did this happen?

In the days, weeks, and months that followed his death, I learned of a past that Rob's family never talked about. My husband was not the first. His was one of many suicides that spanned generations.

My life changed the day that Rob died. November 8, 2003. Things have never been the same. I was left with three young children to support and raise. The illness that consumed Rob created a new and strange life, a life we never imagined. There were no easy answers. There was no map to guide us.

I pushed through, both for my children and myself. On the journey, I chose to listen to my heart and my instincts. The choices I made in the shadow of Rob's death—decisions made in the trenches of emotional pain—formed me and shaped me.

In the face of devastating loss, it is difficult to comprehend or even imagine the rest of your life. The fog grows thick in an unforeseen reality. What is real? How do I go on? Where do I begin? What comes next? What do I do? I struggled intensely.

Things did not return to normal for me. My life changed. This is my story. This is the story of how I came to understand.

Yet in the world around me, I saw no trace of the emotion and fear that rocked my world after Rob's death. The loss struck me with the precision of a thunderbolt. A hovering cloud of depression shadowed me. But everything around me continued apace. People seemed the same. Life moved on. But not for me.

Even time spent with friends amounted to little more than simply shared moments. Fleeting. Temporary. A wrinkle in time surrounded by pain. These friends returned to their normal lives and routines. I felt the hole from the loss long into the night and in the early hours of the morning. The emotional wound abided in the core of my being. It festered. It grew. It hurt.

Things did not return to normal for me. My life changed. This is my story. This is the story of how I came to understand.

one
letter

DEAR FRIENDS

New beginnings are often disguised as painful endings.

—*Tao Te Ching*

December 31, 2003

Dear Friends,

It is New Year's Eve, and I'm thinking of how different 2004 will be for me, Chase, Whitney, and Maddie. A year ago, at this time, we were skiing at Boyne Mountain with friends and spent the evening at our favorite Petoskey restaurant, Chandlers. We started 2003 on a high note, full of hope and expectation. Today, I'm confused, scared, and saddened by our tremendous loss. Now, each day is taken moment by moment. We constantly look for peace and understanding.

It is amazing to me that through these difficult times I have been able to find some peace and comfort. Thank you for your support and care: phone calls, letters, cards, and emails. I have received gifts and acts of kindness from people I don't even know, each wanting me to know they feel for the kids and me. The wonderful meals that have been delivered to our door fed our bellies and warmed our souls. We have been showered with gifts and acts of kindness. A high school friend shared a copy of a poem, faded and edges torn, that he had kept in his wallet for twenty years. All the donations in Rob's honor will truly make a difference to the Land Conservancy and the Make-A-Wish Foundation.

3

i understand

I want to thank each one of you; you have helped make a difference to my family and me too. Everything said and done during these past eight weeks—no matter how big or how small—has impacted us. I will always remember that you were there for us.

I wish I could have given each of you a hug at the memorial service. Unfortunately, I couldn't talk with most of you. However, simply knowing you were there meant so much.

We carry so many memories of Rob with us. I was fortunate to have Rob in my life for almost twenty years. We lived, loved, and experienced life together. Rob had a fulfilled and happy life. He was proud of his family and all they have accomplished. It was a surprise to many of you to learn that Rob struggled with depression. To most people who knew him, he seemed fine. A man who had it all! Although I knew pieces of his internal struggles and the battles that raged within, I did not see this coming. Rob's depression reached darker places, the depths of which I did not understand.

Please move forward with us and remember Rob for the way he lived and the type of special person he was.

In our years together, I learned so many things from Rob. It is because of him that I am the person I am today. Rob taught me to live with no regrets. I have learned the difference between conditional and unconditional love. I have also learned that there are always people that have more than you, but many more people have less. Help the ones with less. I have learned not to judge others.

As a family missing one key member, we move forward now, holding onto our memories. We learn and understand more each day. Chase, fifteen years old, will continue to move towards a black belt in Tae Kwon Do. He enjoys his job at the Forest Hills Public Schools Food Service facility. He continues to take pride in learning

4

about photography and playing his guitar. Whitney, twelve years old, will be starting classes at the Civic Theatre after taking the fall session off for cheerleading. She is also taking tennis lessons so her mom can have a tennis partner. Maddie, a mere five years old, will continue with her Daisy Scouts in hopes to earn all of her "pedals." Her dancing and skating will keep her busy on her "off" school days. My job is obvious: parenting alone is both my biggest challenge and greatest priority. I will do whatever is needed to ensure Chase, Whitney, and Maddie have a fulfilled and successful life.

Please move forward with us and remember Rob for the way he lived and the type of special person he was.

Love,

Vonnie

STARTING OVER

*I know how much you miss me—I see the pain inside your heart;
but I'm not so far away. We really aren't apart.*

—*Author unknown*

On December 31, 2003, six weeks after Rob's death, I sat down and
wrote the letter above. It was mailed out to hundreds of family members, friends, and business associates. I never imagined I would be
a widow at the age of thirty-nine. More shocking than just being a
widow was that I was one because of suicide. That letter was my first
step to survive and move forward. As I read the words now, I realize
that I put on a good face. My words masked much of the pain. Despite the strength of my words, I was left with so much confusion,
guilt, shame, and sadness. I didn't know where to turn or what to do.
I had so many questions. What happened? What *really* happened?
Why did Rob do this? How does someone who seems to have it all
get to a place of wanting to end it all?

Our family name, Woodrick, was (and is) well-known throughout western Michigan. It is associated with a very successful business
founded by Rob's family. We were public figures on a small stage. Big
fish in a small pond. That made Rob's death—a deeply personal and
family matter—a public event.

Friends and strangers responded in various ways, some negatively
and some positively. Gossip and rumors flew around our community.
My late husband, my children, and I were the object of verbal sport.
Our names were tossed from one person to the next, sullied by in-

nuendo and imagination. The questions and concern were constant. Some jarred us with their tone of accusation: "Was this his first attempt?" Or, "How did he do it?" I was often left speechless.

Despite this seemingly unending chatter, others acted and spoke in more helpful and gracious ways. The outpouring of support was unbelievable. So many people reached out and wanted to help in whatever way they could. They brought food, took the kids for outings, or just talked. People graciously shared their own stories of suicide's effect on those they knew and loved. They wanted to know how the kids and I were doing. They asked, "How are you holding up?" Or, "What can we do to help?"

Each time a friend dropped off a meal, I felt the need to explain how wonderful Rob was. I felt the need to defend him. I praised him. I told people what a great husband and a great father he was. I said that no one could ever love me as much as Rob did. I talked about his incredible love for the kids. I explained that the family finances were in order and that Rob had been strong and healthy. I put on a good show, for myself and for others.

Yet I felt as if everywhere I went people were pointing, staring, whispering, and talking. The whispers echoed. People I didn't even know would offer condolences, reach out to hug me, or give me sympathetic looks. Little did

My life stood still, not ready to move forward because it had to move forward without Rob.

they know that it made it worse; it made me want to break down and cry, which I usually did. I needed help and support. Yet I didn't want help and support. I wanted my old life back!

Generous as it was, the outpouring of support only lasted a few months. The season passed, at least for others. People moved on. New tragedies and fresh drama averted the gaze. I came to understand and accept that people's sympathy has a quick expiration date. It was difficult at first. It felt like people were silently saying, "You've had enough time to grieve; pick yourself up and move on." Their lives had not changed, and most of them had no idea what it was like to lose the most important person in their lives.

But how could I move on? I didn't want to.

My life stood still, not ready to move forward because it had to move forward without Rob.

two

fairy tale

A SMALL-TOWN GIRL

Just a small-town girl, livin' in a lonely world.

—Journey

Life was simpler once. I was born in Grand Rapids, Michigan, at Osteopathic Hospital—today known as Metro Hospital—to John and Jean Savela. Both of my parents were from a small town called Mass City, in the Upper Peninsula of Michigan. It was an old mining town, and many residents worked in the copper mines in the surrounding areas. Many Finlanders settled in this area; my dad's family was among them.

My childhood was filled with love and family. I spent time with cousins, aunts, and uncles. My mom had a huge family with seven brothers and sisters; my dad's family was large too—two brothers and three stepsiblings. As a family, we held on to Finnish traditions, especially pasties—meat pies made with potatoes, rutabaga, carrots, and onions—a favorite meal with a history. Family always mattered.

At first, we lived in a trailer park in Cutlerville, a small town outside of Grand Rapids. Humble beginnings. Beyond a faint memory of riding my tricycle up and down the sidewalk, I don't remember much about those years.

When I was very little, my mom worked in a cookie factory, Holland American Wafer Company. I recall stopping into the factory at times with my mom. The smell of warmth, sweetness, and cookies filled the air. My uncle, the factory manager, would always welcome us with a sheet of wafers. That was a highlight of my visits.

i understand

Later my mom went to work for Rochester Products, a division of General Motors. She worked the first shift, which meant she was up at the crack of dawn and out the door hours before I awoke. My dad worked the second shift at another General Motors factory. He left before my mom returned home. My older sister, Candy, and I were fortunate enough to only need a babysitter for about an hour a day to bridge the gap in our parents' work schedules. Like ships passing in the night, my parents traded spaces between home and work to raise us. Before the rust began to settle on the Rust Belt, my parents were part of the American industrial machine—a blue-collar family. My parents worked hard; nothing was given to them. They were kind people, the most sincere and selfless people you would ever meet: humble, hardworking, honest.

When I was four years old, my parents built a home in Caledonia, Michigan, a small, sleepy community dubbed "Cow Town" by the locals. Our home was a modest three-bedroom house with an in-ground pool and a sauna, a Finnish tradition. The house was their pride and joy. I attended Kettle Lake Elementary School—the name says it all. At the time, my world was so very small, and everything seemed so far away. In the winter, the snow covered the ground as far as the eye could see; by summer, the snow was replaced with the golden glow of cornfields. Things moved at a slow pace. There were no cell phones. There was no internet. It seems now like such a faraway place.

Memories of those days still seem like the present in my mind. I remember buying worms and candy from a little gray-haired man on my way to fish at Thornapple River with my dad. We fished for hours. Catch and release, catch and release. Precious memories.

As a child, I was always a daddy's girl. Wherever he was, that is where I wanted to be. I was his little shadow and simply couldn't pass up a chance to go to a garage sale or auction with him. He would say, "One man's junk is another man's treasure."

My mom was dedicated and hardworking. She always showed her love through food, a most delicious way of caring. Providing meals was her love language (the same is true today). I have always admired and respected her.

My sister and I are two and a half years apart. I was the typical little sister: annoying her, borrowing her clothes, tagging along with her and her friends, and yes, even pulling her hair.

However, we weren't the Cleavers of *Leave It to Beaver* fame by any stretch of the imagination. Our life was not a portrait of perfection. My mom and dad both worked. There were struggles, hardships, and disagreements. My dad—although sober now for over thirty years—struggled with overindulging in the bottle, a painful thing to watch.

Neither parent could attend school parties or pick me up after classes. I was always the kid without a parent at school functions. Although I wished my parents could have been present more, I never wanted for anything. Every night, there was a hot meal on the table, courtesy of the slow cooker. We were a typical middle-class, dual-income family.

Life was, well, simple. Simple is good.

In high school, I hung out with every group and was an active member of the Future Farmers of America, which was odd for someone who didn't actually live on a farm. I was vice president of the student body during my junior and senior years, and I was on the yearbook staff. I loved being involved in as many groups as I could.

I remember being elected to the homecoming court in my junior year. My mom bought me a new dress and heels. As I rode in the convertible in the parade, I kept looking for my parents. They weren't there; they were working. The boy who accompanied me that day—everyone called him Captain—chose to take someone else (!) to the homecoming dance. As a result, I skipped the dance. Instead, my friend took me to Mr. Fables, a restaurant where we both worked. We ordered French fries and chocolate milkshakes and talked for hours while dipping our fries into the milkshakes. All while still in my dress!

For my high school graduation, I was handed honor cords. That genuinely surprised me. I never gave myself enough credit to be a stellar student. I worked hard, but schoolwork never came easy for me. Socializing was easy.

Like so many people as they walk across the stage, I had no idea of what the months, years, and decades ahead held in store. Life was, well, simple. Simple is good.

ROB

To be brave is to love someone unconditionally.

—Author unknown

I recall looking through photo books of Rob as a child. I loved seeing him in his white judo outfit with a bowl cut and a huge smile on his face. Judo was a family affair as his dad, Bob, his mom, Aleicia, and sister, Georgia, would all head to the dojo. I knew this was an important time in Rob's life. He valued family time in competition and the weekends spent together. Even as an adult he would speak highly of his judo master, Stan.

Rob developed passions for many things at an early age. He preferred skiing and motocross to baseball and football. One of his friends told me that Rob's dad coached their baseball team. He carpooled with Rob and his dad to practice, but Rob usually wasn't in the car or at practice, even though his dad was a coach. Typical Rob! Once, Rob was signed up for ski racing camp, but he told the camp leaders that there was a mistake and he was supposed to attend the freestyle ski camp. On another occasion, he was put on a sailboat for sailing camp; he didn't want to be there, so he jumped off and swam to shore. That was Rob—determined, a pursuer of his own passions. He wanted to do what he wanted to do.

His love for fishing came at an early age. His best memories of youth were fishing with his grandpa, Bing, at Big Star Lake, north of Grand Rapids. His grandpa's creel had a prominent place in his office.

Learning didn't come easy for him. He struggled but managed to get by. He graduated from Forest Hills Northern High School. He really struggled with numbers. However, aided by determination and technology, he pushed past his learning hurdles. Looking back, I wonder if Rob should've followed his dream of becoming a marine biologist, living in a warm place and studying each day surrounded by the beauty, nature, and intrigue of the sea. Instead, Rob followed in the footsteps of his family. He graduated from Western Michigan University with a degree in food distribution, completed an internship program in Paris with a large grocery chain, and then started working in one of the family stores.

Rob loved the grocery business his grandfather founded, D&W Food Centers. As a child, he relished joining his father at the stores on Sunday afternoons when they were closed. They would stop by several locations, and he would ride grocery carts down the aisles or help himself to a big pickle from the jar on the meat counter. He recalled his grandfather cutting meat and said the meat department was known for having the best cuts in town. Being the third generation in the business, he wanted to make his father proud and carry on the family name in the company.

Rob started at the bottom at D&W; he began work as a bag boy. Rob bagged groceries and carried them out to cars for customers. At that time, the company had ten stores and was known as a higher-end grocery store compared to other supermarkets in the community. The décor, cleanliness, and customer service at D&W outshined the others.

The company motto came from Rob's dad: "At D&W you can never do too much for the customer." This motto was printed out, framed, and placed by every phone, every advertisement.

Rob quickly moved up the corporate ladder in the family business, and before long he was an executive. However, it was not easy for Rob to be the "SOB," as he would say—the son of the boss.

I wouldn't understand until years later the impact it had on him. Rob put a lot of pressure on himself to prove his dedication and worth. He was always first at the office, arriving before 7 a.m., and he was the last to leave. He wanted all the office associates to see his hard work. Rob so tried to demonstrate his worth in a business world in which others sought promotions but he would get them. It was a world where others watched for him to make mistakes and enjoyed watching him fail. He didn't want anyone to think he was receiving any favors because of who he was. Rob wanted to be acknowledged for the work he was doing and who he was as a person, not for being the boss's son.

HAPPENSTANCE

There are chance meetings with strangers that interest us from the first moment, before a word is spoken.

—*Fyodor Dostoevsky*

I was nineteen years old and attending a local college, where I befriended another student. We became best friends and dated brothers for a short time. We had so much fun together. She was a year older than me. We looked alike and acted like sisters.

We would go to the local college hangout, although I wasn't old enough to get in. We had a plan that never failed us: my friend and our acquaintance would go in; the acquaintance would then come back out to give me my friend's ID so I could pass as my friend to get into the club. The place, Electric Avenue, was where all the local college kids went. It wasn't really my thing, though, as I was never into the bar or party scene. I served as the designated driver, or my friends just stopped asking me to go as they realized I wasn't enjoying my time there.

My friend was working in the D&W corporate office as a receptionist, and I was a cashier at a local mom-and-pop grocery store, Boorsma Foods. She encouraged me to apply at D&W, and I did. I was soon working as a cashier at a new location in my hometown of Caledonia.

One day, my friend told me that she had met Rob upon his return from an internship in France. While abroad, he worked in a family grocery store for about six months. Upon his return to the States, Rob became the produce manager for one of the D&W stores.

One evening, we decided to stop at the location where Rob worked. We didn't go there to see him, but rather to visit our friend who also worked there. But fate had its ways. I was walking down the wine aisle when I heard our friend approach. I turned, causing my purse to swing widely, knocking a bottle off the shelf. It shattered on the floor. I stood there with my mouth open, embarrassed and in shock. Rob arrived, carrying a mop and bucket.

That was our first meeting. The stars aligned over shattered glass and spilled wine on the floor of a grocery store. The butterfly effect! A mere happenstance set my life on a different course. That accident in a grocery store aisle changed everything.

I apologized profusely. I am sure my face was bright red. We quickly exited the store, leaving Rob to take care of my mess.

The next day, my friend called me. Her words surprised me. Rob had come by her office that day to inquire about me! He indicated that he would like to ask me out. My friend asked me if I would accept. Although Rob was cute and I was intrigued, I said there was no way. I couldn't imagine myself dating the son of the owner. I was just a small-town girl from Caledonia.

A mere happenstance set my life on a different course.

Later, the friend whom we had gone to visit told my friend that Rob had promised her a job for life on one condition—that he get my phone number. She eagerly passed it along without even asking me.

Unaware of what was going on, I called my friend that same day to make plans for Friday evening. She was busy, so I was considering other options when the phone rang. It was my friend calling me back to tell me that I should expect a call from Rob. She had informed him that I was free on Friday night.

I was mortified. I did not want to go on a date with him. I liked my simple life, and I worried that I might lose my job if he didn't like me or if the date was bad.

Well, he called, and I went. On our first date, Rob picked me up in his mother's convertible. We drove out to the shore of Lake Michigan and walked the pier on a beautiful summer night while the waves splashed against the shoreline. We ate pizza at a quaint restaurant—Fricanos in Holland, Michigan—that had red and white checked tablecloths and a line out the door. Perfect first date!

LOVE

In the end there doesn't have to be anyone who understands you. There just has to be someone who wants to.

—*Robert Brault*

From the beginning of our date, we felt at ease with each other, as if we had known each other for a long time. It did not take long before we were smitten; there was a connection between us that told me we were meant to be. The attraction was instant! His knowledge, soft heart, and kindness all swept me off my feet.

Rob was very attractive. And he was as kind as he was good looking. Admittedly, I hesitated because Rob and I came from two totally different worlds. He was much more sophisticated and worldly than I was. He loved to cook for us while listening to jazz, drinking wine, and dancing throughout the kitchen. He was fun, down to earth, and so trusting.

Rob loved to ski; I hadn't skied a day in my life. I remember early on in our relationship a trip to Boyne Mountain in northern Michigan. I was an avid ice skater, so I had good balance. I made it down the bunny hill with ease, so Rob told me that I was a natural at skiing. I think back about that moment and laugh now. He immediately brought me to the face of the mountain and said, "You can do this!" Well . . . I couldn't, and I proceeded to go down the black diamond on my butt, sliding all the way to the base of the mountain.

He was active and adventurous, and I admired that as he kept me busy by always teaching me new things. Rob always had a lot of faith in me, assuming that I could do what he could do with ease. The truth was that I was shy, quiet, and a bit reserved, so these new adventures became somewhat stressful. I loved shopping in Chicago or going to fancy restaurants. I was not, however, used to going to the places Rob and his family went to.

I learned early on to forgo shrimp cocktail (that was too basic), to say no to a doggie bag if you couldn't eat all your food, to appreciate that certain gourmet foods—such as caviar—were an acquired taste. I learned each of these things from Rob's family. Frankly, I couldn't comprehend why someone would like caviar, sea urchin, or sweetbread (an organ from an animal). What I couldn't figure out is why on earth we would have to "acquire" a taste for something before we could enjoy it.

He needed me in ways I couldn't begin to understand.

Rob's parents had a condo in Marco Island, Florida. We really enjoyed traveling there to spend time with his parents. It was there that we began our tradition of deep-sea fishing and eating our catch. Rob was a certified scuba diver, so I earned my certification as well. Snorkeling and diving became favorite pastimes. We also looked forward to stone crab season, key lime pie, and visits to the Goodland Fish House. These were the best of times.

Something else also drew me to Rob, an unexplainable sense of compassion toward him. I knew we were meant to be together, but not for the reasons I would have thought. I felt as if he needed someone to take care of him. I felt many misunderstood his efforts to constantly prove himself. Was he insecure because of the expectations he put on himself? Did his family misunderstand him? Did he really want to work in the family business?

Once I got to know Rob, I knew that I could never walk away from the man I fell in love with. I knew he needed me; this strong feeling assured me we would be together for a lifetime. He needed me in ways I couldn't begin to understand. I would soon find out about some of those ways.

On October 11, 1986, after two years of dating, we wed.

WORDS

But they all didn't see the little bit of sadness in me.

—Kid Cudi

Married two years after we met, Rob and I seemed to be a perfect pair. We had so much love and respect for each other. At the same time, I had so much compassion for him. He had so many internal struggles—hidden battles in his mind. I was a cheerleader to him on the days he thought the sky was falling. I was his rock. I believe the unconditional love I shared with him made him love me even more.

We always celebrated our anniversary in Chicago, usually at the Four Seasons or the Park Hyatt. One anniversary, I was out shopping and believed he was doing his usual tour of restaurants throughout the day. However, on this day, he asked me to meet him at noon outside the hotel. We walked to a door next to the hotel, and he rang the bell. The gates opened, and we were welcomed in with a glass of champagne waiting for each of us. I was suddenly standing inside Sidney Garber, a high-end jewelry store. I was guided to a counter where four rings were presented. "Happy anniversary!" Rob said, along with, "Pick one." I was stunned and speechless. I couldn't do it; the rings were far too glamorous for me. I asked for another glass of champagne to calm my nerves. As I walked around the store, Rob followed me and said, "You can choose anything; it doesn't have to be one that I chose for you."

I finally chose one. The diamond ring was so sparkly, beautiful, and amazing. Rob raised his glass of champagne and said, "Happy tenth anniversary!" I hesitated and smiled. I raised my glass and said, "Happy ninth anniversary!" We looked at each other and started laughing. I said something like, "Can't wait to see what our *actual* tenth anniversary will bring!"

A year later, on our true ten-year anniversary, we were back in Chicago, having a great time at our favorite places. When we dined, the staff often treated Rob like he was a food critic, a reputation he earned. Dining was an experience with Rob; his knowledge of food and wine far surpassed the average person's. We frequently received complimentary appetizers or wine samples. Somehow, Rob often made his way into the kitchen of the restaurant.

Rob loved art galleries. He could spend hours moving from frame to frame. One of his favorite artists was Markus Pierson. He enjoyed checking out Pierson's latest pieces at the Merrill Chase Gallery. To our surprise, Pierson happened to be at the gallery that day. That is where Rob chose my tenth anniversary gift.

The piece was named *The Perfect Pair*, and the caption stated in part:

"To them the other was much like a common pear—full of imperfections and yet perfect in its entirety. They adored one another in spite of the changes and evolutions they encountered, as this was just the further ripening of a pear and oh what beauty nature does put on view. Of course, a little nibbling is nice too. If only to validate authenticity."

Pierson signed the piece, and my heart is still touched by this meaningful gift: "Happy Anniversary to the perfect pair."

I recall sitting across from Rob's desk week after week, enamored by his wisdom and the love he had for so many people—most importantly his family. My heart was so soft for him because I also witnessed his constant anxiety and earnest effort.

PERFECT

The really happy person is one who can enjoy the scenery when on a detour.

—*Author unknown*

Rob was a world traveler, yet his favorite place on earth was our summer home just outside of Boyne City, a picturesque place in northern Michigan perched on the southeast end of Lake Charlevoix, which cuts a long, thin swath of blue on the map near the top of the famed Michigan mitten.

Rob loved the outdoors, and it was only after he passed that I truly appreciated the beauty surrounding our cottage; it was a special place, one where I enjoyed spending time with my family and friends but also the place where my healing began.

One August day as our family was frolicking on the shores of Horton Bay, I had a moment. It was a moment that didn't appear often, but on that day it was clear and present.

I was standing on the dock. To my left Whitney and Maddie were splashing in the clear water on the sandy shore; to my right Chase was in a canoe with his friend. Straight ahead, Rob was sailing on a beautiful, breezy, sunny day. It was perfect. Everything was just right. We were all in the same place within several hundred feet of each other enjoying this summer day. It was a scene of serenity. A cherished moment.

When we spent time in northern Michigan, it was our chance to decompress from all the worries and busyness of school and work.

Horton Bay was a special place. We only had local TV and no internet. It was so important to Rob for the kids to be outside enjoying nature and learning the history of the area. We did all the family things: staying in a cottage, playing games, swinging in hammocks, roasting marshmallows around a bonfire, playing monkey in the middle on the beach, and welcoming friends. Our home had a revolving front door of friends coming and going. My fondest memories of Rob, the kids, and our family are there.

three
tragedy

SPIRAL

Your biggest hurdle isn't your opponent, it is yourself.

—Brandon Todd

When he was thirty-two, I told Rob he had the job of a man in his fifties. He was an executive. We traveled; we had a beautiful home, nice cars, and money to buy and do whatever we wanted. But Rob was not happy. He disagreed with the direction the company was headed. Other members of the family became frustrated with him. Amid the tension, Rob decided to leave the family business.

Walking away was difficult for him. He left what he loved and the business he was so passionate about. He struggled with direction while considering different business options. During this stressful season of life, his anxiety and agitation increased. I found myself walking on eggshells around him so that he would not lose his temper.

His anxiety became so great that we realized he needed medication. That helped; the change in his behavior was clear and demonstrable. When he stopped taking his medicine, it was obvious. The anxiety and agitation returned. He would become restless and show signs of muddled thinking. At times, Rob thought and acted as if the sky was falling.

Rob ultimately remained in the food business, but he decided to switch from groceries to restaurants. It seemed to be a natural transition for Rob. He opened a restaurant in downtown Grand Rapids in 1996. He poured his heart and soul into Bistro Bella Vita. The restaurant was beautiful. Rob came back to life again. He was proud of his restaurant. Its staff was professionally trained, it had the city's first martini bar, and it served outstanding food. It opened at the same time as the Van Andel Arena—an 11,000-seat multipurpose venue, in the heart of Grand Rapids. The new arena was right across the street from Rob's new restaurant. A perfect location. When the Van Andel Arena held an event, the restaurant was packed. The atmosphere buzzed with good food, excellent wine, and wonderful company.

Rob's new business was thriving, but he started to question the size of the restaurant. He feared that the restaurant was maybe too big for what downtown needed at that time. Worry began to consume him as he wondered about this. He wondered if the restaurant was too dependent on the arena for foot traffic. Would people go to the restaurant if there was no event at the arena? Was the restaurant itself enough of a draw? Rob's anxiety started to peak again. He started indulging in martinis too often.

By that point, we had been going to counseling for years. Rob struggled with his departure from the family business and with his overwhelming need for approval from his parents. In counseling, we would talk about Rob's drinking. The psychologist did not believe that he had a drinking problem, but he did question Rob's use of alcohol as a form of self-medication.

Despite the hurdles and his own mental struggles, Rob pushed on. He poured time, money, and energy into the restaurant. He was determined to succeed. Five years later, on Rob's fortieth birthday, a second Bistro Bella Vita opened in another area of Grand Rapids. He also opened a small specialty wine and food market in Ada, Michigan, outside of Grand Rapids. He called it Market Bella Vita.

Then came September 11, 2001. The terrorist attacks in New York City devastated the nation. Rob took the events of that day particularly hard; they triggered him. The days that followed were particularly dark and difficult for him. The staggering losses of human life profoundly affected Rob. He also started worrying more and more about the economy and the future. He feared people would stop going out to eat and would stop spending money on specialty food items. Rob thought he was going to lose everything he worked so hard to achieve. His fears crippled him. He would lie in bed curled up in a ball for days upon days.

Our family psychologist came to the house, talked with Rob, and helped him out of this dark state through counseling. But amid this depression and anxiety, Rob left both restaurants and the market. He felt like an absolute failure. He was so hard on himself.

I watched Rob lose the self-confidence and passion that I so admired.

Rob slowly climbed out of the dark hole of his mind and the crippling depression. Things started to improve. With medical attention, his immediate family's love, and his extended family's support, he got better, day by day. Rob then wanted to return to managing and working on the restaurants and the market, but that was not an option.

Rob struggled over what to do next. He possessed great foresight and the ambition to do something. But what? He had plenty of ideas—some great and some not so great—but nothing he thought of resulted in anything. He developed a powerful fear of failure.

During this time, I tried to listen to his needs and concerns. I was a cheerleader and reassured him that everything would be fine. I wanted him to take some time to focus on himself and the kids, and eventually he did. He became a dad involved in every aspect of his children's lives. He wanted to take them everywhere and do everything with them. He immersed himself in their lives.

Unfortunately, Rob wasn't feeling fulfilled. He wanted another business, but since nothing was coming to fruition, he continued to feel like a failure and began to think that he was becoming a burden to us. I couldn't understand his thought process. It didn't make sense to me.

I encouraged him to look beyond a new career or business and instead to work with kids and make a difference in the lives of the less fortunate. It didn't matter if he got paid or had a title. He loved working with children, but that wasn't enough for him. Rob wanted more; he was driven to want more.

It was a sad time for me. I watched Rob lose the self-confidence and passion that I so admired. I was confused, alone, hurt, and afraid. What was happening? My life—our life!—felt like it was unraveling. Rob was spiraling into a deeper and darker hole of depression, one from which he wouldn't emerge.

ACT

Peace of mind is attained not by ignoring problems, but by solving them.

—Raymond Hull

At 8:20 in the morning on November 4, 2003, the phone rang. As I reached to pick it up, I heard my husband, Rob, say from the other room that he was going outside. I thought nothing of it; he was probably going to feed the dog.

My phone conversation lasted less than five minutes; it was the school principal calling about a student Rob had taken under his wing. The student was a friend of our son who had lost his dad years ago and whose mom was in jail. He was one of three boys Rob was mentoring at the time. After I hung up, I quickly checked on my five-year-old daughter, Maddie, then went to see what Rob was up to outside. I opened the front door and called to him.

"Rob?"

My voice hung in the air, suspended by the silence without reply. I felt a small spike of panic in my stomach; something was wrong. I ran through the house looking for him, and, as I heard my voice calling his name, it sounded distant, as if I were listening to myself from under a shallow pool of water.

He wasn't in the house.

As I approached the door to our lower garage, I noticed it was unlocked; this was strange. I rushed forward, propelled by a sense of dread quickly spreading in my chest, and pulled open the door. It was black; the lights were off. I stared into the expanding darkness and yelled his name, again.

"ROB?"

As I turned to go upstairs, the unlocked door loomed uneasily in my mind, so I turned back. I opened it once more, flipped on the switch, and my world shifted. There he was: Rob, my husband, the father of my children, hanging by a rope attached to the garage door. For a moment, time slowed to a near standstill, and then I started moving very quickly.

It was black; the lights were off. I stared into the expanding darkness and yelled his name, again.

The panic in my stomach surged into my chest. I ran to him, sure of only one thing: I couldn't leave him there. I wrapped my arms around his torso, struggling to lift him to ease the pressure away from his neck. But he was too heavy, too high up. I was wasting time—precious, precious time. I ran into the house and called 911.

I ran back into the garage to open the door so the paramedics could get to him as quickly as possible, but the rope Rob tied to it wouldn't allow it to open. There was just enough room for me to crawl under it. I slid under the door, feeling my knees scrape the concrete, and ran up the driveway. Sirens wailed in the distance, getting louder as they came closer.

In the few minutes since I had found Rob, time had slowed, cruelly so, and each moment that passed lessened his chances of survival.

My mind reeled, repeating, "How can this be happening? Why is this happening?"

Within minutes, the driveway was flooded with firefighters, paramedics, and police officers. They were calm, as they are trained to be, and worked swiftly while my life shattered. I'm not even sure when

I called his parents and my parents, but they were both there soon after.

Rob lay on the cold garage floor while paramedics started CPR and worked to revive him. At that point, both my parents and Rob's had arrived, his mother insisting that she needed to see him. I would not let her; I didn't want anyone to see Rob lying on the garage floor in this state.

My mother took Maddie into our room, kept her from what was happening, and let her world remain as she had always known it, for a little while longer.

I was overcome with hysteria—this was not my life; this was not happening. This was a horror movie; this was not real. I tried to will the world to go back as it was. It did not.

A firefighter named Dave sat with me as my heart raced, a Morse code of shock.

"Is he alive?" I cried. "Is he alive? I just want to know if he is alive. I just need to know."

He was, Dave told me. My relief at this was met with concern. What now? What's next?

I was in shock, my body was numb, and my new reality was quickly approaching.

Moments later, I was riding in the car with my in-laws, following the ambulance to the hospital.

I was in shock, my body was numb, and my new reality was quickly approaching.

HOSPITAL

We must be willing to let go of the life we planned so as to have the life that is waiting for us.

—*Joseph Campbell*

We soon arrived at the hospital and were brought to a waiting room. Someone came out and handed me a bag of Rob's clothes. I thought this was strange. Why were they giving me clothes? Where was he? What did they put on him? Why couldn't I go with him? At that point, my brother-in-law was there, and I handed him the bag and said, "I don't ever want to see these clothes again."

I was in a surreal state. I was at the hospital, but I wasn't there. My mind was someplace else. I was in shock. What was happening felt both real and unreal at the same time.

When I was finally allowed to go to Rob's room, his mother was able to go with me, but we couldn't stay long. Two detectives were waiting to speak with me, so we went with them. The room was dark, the lights were off, and I was reminded of suspenseful interrogation scenes in movies. But it wasn't someone else under scrutiny. I was the target of their questions.

"Has your husband ever tried anything like this before?"

"Who was home?"

"Where were you?"

"Where did he get the rope?"

Rob's act was deeply disturbing for me, and the cold, repetitive interrogation exacerbated the horror. I was unnerved. They asked me the same thing over and over as if I would change my response. Finally, my mother-in-law said enough was enough. They left, and we both returned to Rob's room in ICU.

The hospital chaplain made his way to us to ask if we could all pray together. We sat and prayed. We talked about Rob and other families he helped in similar situations.

It was difficult to see Rob lying there so helpless. He had a bright rope burn on his neck—a jarring reminder of what had put him there. I neatly folded a washcloth and placed it on his neck.

I commented that he seemed very cold and that I would bring a blanket for him from home.

The chaplain said they had blankets made by different guild members and he would get one for Rob. He asked us what Rob liked to do—maybe he could find a blanket that reflected that. Rob's mom and I both said he liked fishing and skiing. I told the chaplain that if he couldn't find one with fishing or skiing on it, red was Rob's favorite color.

It didn't take long for the chaplain to return with a blanket with red hot-air balloons on it.

I draped it over Rob and said to him, "I've covered you with a blanket with hot-air balloons. That is something we have never done. When you get better, we'll go for a hot-air balloon ride."

At that moment, I felt satisfied. I truly felt he knew I was there and felt a connection with the hope of going on a hot-air balloon ride together.

The next day, I brought pictures of the kids and set them up in the room. I desperately wanted Rob to wake up and see his children. It was parent-teacher conference time at their schools, which I had obviously missed, but I brought the report cards to his room. In tears, I went over each one of their grades with him. A part of me believed Rob could hear me and was listening.

Surprising us all, Rob opened his eyes. I felt so much excitement and hope; I just kept talking, wanting so badly that they would stay open. The nurse was in the room and told me it was a common reflex for someone in a coma. Each time his eyes flickered, I jumped up and started talking. I wanted to believe he could hear what I was saying. I wanted him to know I was there. I wanted him to know how much we all loved him.

At one point, as his eyes were open, I looked into them and felt as if I heard him say, "I'm sorry, Von."

It was another surreal moment. I heard those words loud and clear with nothing being said. The room itself was silent.

As the minutes turned into hours, I came to accept that Rob wasn't coming home.

That evening, I gathered our children around me and told them their dad probably wouldn't be coming home.

That evening, I gathered our children around me and told them their dad probably wouldn't be coming home. My heart shattered as their tears flowed. I asked the older two not to share the circumstances of his death with Maddie.

Two days later, Rob still had made no progress, and the doctors told us it was time to take him off the ventilator, after which one of two things would happen: he would either breathe on his own and potentially live with brain damage due to lack of oxygen, or he would pass quietly.

As the doctors explained the possible outcomes to me, I thought about what our lives would be like if he lived. How much care would he need? How cognitive would he be? Would he be in a vegetative state? I knew he didn't want to live in those conditions. Perhaps selfishly, I wondered how I could do it all. I pictured him in that state and prayed for peace for Rob.

Within minutes after the ventilator was turned off, Rob quietly left us. It was November 8, 2003. He was at peace. His anxiety, self-doubt, and depression were gone.

I had to tell our children. That was the hardest conversation I have ever had. Their dad was gone. My heart broke into a million pieces.

On the outside, I was a pillar of strength, yet on the inside I was scared and worried about what the future held.

How could we ever pick up those pieces of our hearts and make them whole again?

TWO SIMPLE WORDS

You will never understand the pain of ignorance until it happens to you.

—*Author unknown*

Rob stood on an edge. He had a decision to make. I now understand that his decision that day was not made with a clear mind. Rob was sick, plagued by doubt, anxiety, and depression. His thinking was compromised.

Earlier, I mentioned the art of Markus Pierson. In a collection of paintings, the Coyote Series, Pierson depicts coyotes, dressed as human beings, in a variety of different situations. *Two Simple Words*, one of his most arresting and disturbing works of art, visually captures Roger O. Hegbarth, a coyote in business attire, standing on the edge of a skyscraper. The following text explains the art:

> For years Roger O. Hegbarth had toiled away at his job, working late while others left early and arriving early while others slept late. He had his reasons. He hated his job, but he loved Manhattan, loved the Chrysler building especially, and he would often dream of the day his company would promote him to its highrise levels. The company building's top two floors had a clear view of the Chrysler building, and Roger could see clearly the day when his feet would rest quite comfortably on his desk while he gazed at the gleaming spires.

Two simple words changed all of that, though. Two simple words scribbled on a note took all of Roger's work and ambition and hope and desperation and wrapped it carefully in a few sheets of white cloud and flushed it cleanly down the toilet. Two very simple words; You're Fired. Note in hand, Roger O. Hegbarth got up from his desk and walked uptown to the Chrysler building. He managed to sneak past everyone and went out onto one of the grand steel eagles that border the Chrysler, where he planned to leap gracefully to his death.

A gentle but firm wind blew against him. He looked out at all the beauty of the city. No matter, Roger O. Hegbarth's dreams had been crushed like an ant under redwood, like a sardine under an ocean liner run aground. Or had they? He let go of the note and Roger O. Hegbarth lived. He lived to fight on another day, until the day his dream finally came true. Whatever dream that might be. And you know, you just never know. (Peabody Gallery website)

Roger, the fictional character on the canvas, faced a decision. Roger stood on the edge. Roger's feet never left that edge. My Rob—impaired by the illness that waged war inside his mind—also stood on the edge. His feet moved.

My Rob—impaired by the illness that waged war inside his mind— also stood on the edge.

FUNERAL

To laugh often and much; to win the respect of intelligent people
and the affection of children; to earn appreciation of honest
critics and endure the betrayal of false friends; to appreciate
beauty, to find the best in others; to leave the world a bit better,
whether by a healthy child, a garden patch or a redeemed social
condition; to know even one life has breathed easier because
you have lived. This is to have succeeded.

—*Bessie Stanley*

Rob's funeral took place on November 12, 2003, at Fountain Street
Church in Grand Rapids, Michigan.

Throughout our marriage, Rob often told me what he wanted at
his funeral if anything happened to him. I would always listen and
say, "Well, I don't have to worry about that for a long time."

Rob told me he wanted a pine box rather than a typical casket.
He was a nature lover at heart and wanted everything to be very
simple. Rob requested that there be no visitation; he couldn't stand
the thought of such a thing. He wanted everyone's last visual of him
to be of him alive.

I couldn't bear the thought of funeral flowers—the ones with
silk ribbons that said, "Beloved husband and father." While beautiful and thoughtful, they represented death. I banned delivery of all
arrangements at our home and the church. Instead, we adorned the
church with gorgeous wildflowers. Rob's friends made the pine box
in which he was laid to rest. They burned fishing flies on the exterior

of the box and attached Rob's skis and ski boots to it. On top, we spread twigs and wildflowers.

For the front of the program, I chose a silhouette photo of Rob fly-fishing before a beautiful sunset. When I considered words to go with it, I thought about how he lived:

"Live Passionately, Love Immensely, and Laugh Like a Child."

Rob did everything with a passion that I longed to feel myself. He did not merely love; he loved us all immensely. Rob used the word *love* regularly; we knew he loved us. Rob not only laughed like a child but he acted like one so much of the time. The kids adored him for that. He lived fully in spite of his illness.

I chose a photo of Rob in a boat for the inside of the program. It represented Lake Charlevoix and his love of water.

The funeral director gave me a book of poems and inspirational verses that I could choose for the program. I picked the first one I read.

It follows:

I'm Free

Don't grieve for me now I'm Free
I'm following the path that God laid for me
I took his hand, when I heard him call
I turned my back and left it all
I could not stay another day
To laugh, to love, to work or play
Tests left undone, they stay that way
I found that place at the close of day
If parting has left a void
Then fill it with remembered joy

i understand

A friendship shared, a laugh, a kiss
Ah, yes these things I too will miss
Be not burdened now with times of sorrow
I wish you the sunshine of tomorrow
My life's been full, I've savored much
Good friends, good times, a loved one's touch
Perhaps my time, seems all to brief
Don't lengthen it now with undue grief
Lift up your heart and share with me
God wanted me now. He set me free.

—Author unknown

Chase was taking photography lessons at the time, and one of my favorite photos of his was of a path covered with leaves. I included it on the back page of the program and named it: "Path Not Yet Traveled." Underneath it read: "We walk down only with the love we were blessed to share with our very special husband and father. Our lives are forever changed but greatly touched for having Rob in it."

Despite the pain, I am glad that Rob had the kind of funeral he wanted. The program was beautiful. More importantly, it showed who Rob really was. It showed his passions.

Rob's parents and I met with the funeral director and ministers to discuss how the service would flow.

The song "On Eagle's Wings" was to open the services, preceding remembrances by friends. The Scott Bell Trio would then perform "You Can't Always Get What You Want" by the Rolling Stones. It was a song Rob sang constantly. He sang it when the kids begged for something. He sang it to me when I tried to get my way. He sang it as a message to himself. He told me on numerous occasions it would have to be played at his funeral.

Then, the minister would speak, followed by the Lord's Prayer and a benediction, and finally the service would close with the Scott Bell Trio performing "I Hope You Dance" by Lee Ann Womack.

The day of Rob's service was the most difficult one of my life. Attending the funeral of a spouse while watching the kids suffer the loss is one of the most excruciating things anyone can endure. The funeral of a spouse and father who dies by suicide is even harder.

Unanswered questions hung in the air. Guilt, shock, and sadness swirled around me. I was not embarrassed or ashamed of Rob for how he died, and I decided to be very open about his death. Yet I was also deeply confused; this was not the Rob I knew. I did know, however, that I clearly hadn't understood the depth of his pain and illness. That was my hard truth in those days. Despite my interior tumult, I wanted his funeral day to be one when we remembered and celebrated his life.

Unanswered questions hung in the air. Guilt, shock, and sadness swirled around me.

Without the help of medication, I wouldn't have made it through Rob's service. On the morning before his funeral, I took an anti-anxiety pill. Before we left for the church, I took another. I was home alone with the kids that morning and tried to be strong for them as my heart broke repeatedly. I questioned how I would ever get through. We all wore red, Rob's favorite color. Rob's dad had taken Chase to buy a new sports coat, pants, shirt, and shoes. I had taken the girls shopping for their outfits.

To this day, I don't remember much of what took place that morning. I drove us all to the church and have no memory whatso-ever of doing so. I recall being in a room where friends tried to come in but were asked to allow us privacy.

The church filled quickly; over nine hundred people came to Rob's service. The line to get in went around the block, and in the end, it was standing room only. If a memorial service could ever be perfect, this one was. The service was beautiful and moving, and I realized how fortunate I was to have had Rob in my life for as long as I did.

The minister talked about what a pleasure it was to have known Rob. He described Rob as a special person who lived his life by loving his family, sharing himself, mentoring others, appreciating the wonders of nature, and enjoying extreme sports.

While we celebrated Rob's life that day, we were open about the fact that he died by suicide. We did not try to hide the fact that his illness won. Rob had succumbed to the battle that raged within himself. He lost to the illness known as depression.

I quickly went to the restroom after the service to wipe my eyes. It all seemed like another surreal experience. The funeral was real, yet it wasn't. The words were spoken, yet they weren't.

I received people for over two hours; so many wanted to hug me and tell me how sorry they were. We provided lunch after the service, but I never made it to lunch due to the outpouring of support from friends and strangers who waited in that long line to express condolences.

Immediate family members went to the cemetery, where the pine box was lowered into the ground. I didn't think my heart could fracture any more, but in that moment it did.

Then it was over, and so was our life with Rob.

four
grief

CHILDREN

In the end your kids won't remember the fancy toy you bought them. They will remember the time you spent with them.

—*Kevin Heath*

In the days and weeks after the funeral, I struggled to comprehend how a father of three could possibly think his children would be better off without him.

I tried to explain depression and suicide in a way they could each understand at their respective ages. I was anxious about sharing too much. I didn't want to cause further harm. Yet I feared that silence and secrecy would allow the cycle of depression-suicide to continue in the next generation. I spoke openly about it with Chase and Whitney. They seemed to understand that their dad was sick. It was harder with Maddie; she was so young.

They seemed to understand that their dad was sick.

How do kids continue their lives after such a tremendous loss? Rob was not an absent father; he was the opposite! Rob was an active, fun, and loving dad who also mentored other children. All the friends of our kids loved Rob and loved to play with him. According to them, he was the best trampoline-bouncer, storyteller, and flashlight monster.

The end of Rob's life didn't make sense to the adults. How would it make sense to children?

Our children experienced Rob's death in their own ways.

51

i understand

Chase

While Rob was an incredible father, the children also witnessed his struggles. When Rob's anxiety level was high, he would be impatient and short-tempered. At times, he would take his frustrations out in front of them. They watched as he picked up a dinner plate and threw it across the room or smashed the fruit in the fruit bowl with his fists. Chase was a frequent witness to this behavior, in part because he was the oldest but also because anxiety about him was often the cause of Rob's anger. Chase was diagnosed with severe learning disabilities, muscle weaknesses, ADHD, and Asperger's syndrome. Yet it was difficult at times to see his struggles as disabilities. This caused Rob great anxiety, and he sometimes felt he was failing as a father.

Despite the struggles, Rob and Chase adored each other and were extremely close; Chase would say, "My dad is my best friend." Rob did everything possible to help Chase become the best person he could be, assuring Chase success in many things that we did not think were possible. With his father's help and encouragement, Chase became a certified scuba diver, completed a driver's training course, and earned a brown belt in Tae Kwon Do. Without Rob, Chase would not have accomplished those things.

After Rob's death, Chase suffered the most. Grief hit immediately. He was confused and refused therapy.

I've witnessed Chase suffer in many ways throughout his life, but watching him grieve was heartbreaking. The silence of Rob's absence left a screaming gap in Chase's life. After Rob passed, Chase, who was fifteen, tried to be strong and show little emotion. At night, I pretended not to hear him sobbing in the shower. I would often find him sitting on a golf cart in the lower garage where Rob hanged himself. Chase seemed to be somewhere else. He was in a daze, staring at the ceiling.

I grew concerned as he continued to hide his feelings and have angry outbursts. He wouldn't listen to me when I tried to talk with him about his father. He would shout, "My dad is a fucking freak for killing himself!" I wondered how many others believed that about Rob.

Chase's anger grew, and he became verbally abusive to me. He began misbehaving, doing what he wanted when he wanted. Once, he walked down the street in a nearby neighborhood and kicked all the trash cans over. He was drinking and staying out all night. He told me that one night he slept under someone's porch. My heart shattered again as I witnessed this behavior.

Chase was defiant at school, where teachers and administrators had always supported him and helped him as best as they could to deal with his disabilities. Now, they didn't want him around, and he was suspended on a regular basis. I was frustrated: Couldn't they understand why he was acting out? Couldn't they offer help instead of discipline?

Chase hit rock bottom a few years later. The shock and trauma of Rob's death left rapids and torrents, not placid streams, for Chase. Still, he has constantly and bravely struggled to navigate life and cope with the loss.

Whitney

Whitney was twelve years old at the time of her dad's death. There was a part of Whitney that loved all the attention and support she received from friends and their families in the wake of Rob's death. I am forever grateful for those who took her under their wings during this very difficult time. It was also a welcome relief to me as I tried to support Chase, who was spiraling downward, and Maddie, who had no idea what had transpired.

Whitney expressed a lot of emotion in the days following her dad's death. She found great comfort in putting her energy into a collage for the memorial service. She had a tremendous support system. Friends who included Whitney and kept her busy allowed her to move forward in a productive and happy way. Whitney also doted on Maddie. With maternal behavior, she showered Maddie with love and affection.

Despite the support from so many people, something I had feared did become real as the days and weeks passed. Some people around us changed. For many extremely religious people, suicide was a sin. For this reason, some people distanced themselves from our family, including from Whitney. The loss of Rob's presence was compounded by the loss of others. The stigma of suicide stained the entire family in the eyes of some. Some people even told Whitney that her father did not go to heaven.

Whitney, like me, struggled with conversation about what happened. What do you say? Do you politely decline to answer questions? Did people act and speak in different ways because of what happened?

Five years after Rob's death, Whitney began to self-medicate with food. Eating comforted her; denying herself food allowed her to be in control. It is a nasty cycle of mind games. She sought help and has been able to let go of the guilt and fear she had due to the loss of her dad.

Maddie

Maddie was five years old and truly a little princess in her daddy's eyes. Because of the age difference between the kids, Rob's relationship with Chase and Whitney was much different than with Maddie. He worked seventy hours a week when the older children were little. When Maddie was born, he was much more flexible and worked from a home office. I watched the relationship between the two of them and thought she was such a blessing. Rob experienced fatherhood in a different way than he had before. He was available to take her to swimming and dance lessons. At her young age, he introduced her to his love of sushi. Maddie was Rob's pure joy. I never saw Rob prouder than when he spent time with Maddie.

After his death, Maddie came home from school one day, and it was evident that she was feeling a little down. I sat with her and asked her what was wrong. She told me that the teacher in gym class talked about the importance of exercise and said the students should encourage their dads to go on walks every night after dinner. Anna, a friend of Maddie's, raised her hand and said, "Maddie doesn't have a dad." I asked Maddie if she responded and she said, "No, I didn't know what to say. It just made me feel bad." I told her that next time anyone made that comment to her she should respond by saying, "I have a dad; everyone has a dad, and mine is in heaven."

Shortly after Rob died, our neighbor asked Maddie if she wanted to go to the daddy-daughter dance with him and his daughter, Bailey. It was the first time I realized how many special things our children would miss out on. Not just shared dances, but also graduations, weddings, grandchildren, and more. My heart still aches with the thought. Maddie didn't go to the dance; her father wasn't there.

One day I dropped Maddie off at a friend's birthday party. The dad was out greeting the kids, with Hawaiian music playing in the background. Buckets were filled with party favors, and grass skirts were wrapped along all the tables. The mom was blending frozen drinks for the kids to sip out of pineapple cups. They were a wonderful family. The parents could always be seen supporting each other, with the dad just as involved in school activities as the mom. I dropped Maddie off and left feeling a tremendous amount of sadness. It made me cry.

Why couldn't Maddie have her dad at her parties? Rob would've been outside greeting and having fun with the kids at her birthday party. It was painful to watch Maddie absorb attention like a sponge from adults, especially her friends' dads. She relished the attention, affection, and fun; but watching her miss out on a relationship with her own father crushed me, over and over.

PAIN

Grief is not a disorder, a disease or sign of weakness. It is an emotional, physical and spiritual necessity, the price you pay for love. The only cure for grief is to grieve.

—Earl Grollman,
Straight Talk about Death for Teenagers

In the days, weeks, months, and even years after Rob's death, our hearts were broken, our lives shattered. The emotions ebbed and flowed. The pain from grief that followed Rob's death was excruciating, debilitating, and exhausting. It was everywhere and all-consuming.

Grief affects adults in different ways. The emotions are raw and visceral. Sometimes you want to cry; at other times you want to scream.

The continued pain after a devastating loss is unimaginable. So many friends and family members told me, "Just get through the first year." I did that. I muddled through that first year in anticipation that things would change. I hoped things would be better—that the pain would stop, the sun would shine again, a smile would return to my face.

The pain from grief that followed Rob's death was excruciating, debilitating, and exhausting.

I was anxious at the end of the first year. I naively had thought something magical was going to happen, that all my pain would be gone and grieving would be done. We would no longer be anticipating the "firsts"—first birthday without him, first Father's Day without him, first Christmas without him, and so on.

But nothing changed. The passing of the first year without Rob did not alleviate the grief. A date on a calendar is not an eraser. Pain was still persistent. Rob was talked about less and less, and the kids still didn't have their dad. I was still very much alone, grieving and trying to figure it all out with a huge hole in my heart.

For me, the second year was harder than the first. Despite all my anticipation, I still felt the same. I still missed him. I still grieved for him, and I was still watching my kids grow up without their dad. What did I miss? What was supposed to change once we got through the first year? Now what do I do? How do we remember him? How do I mark this anniversary of his death—or do I even mark it?

> **I will move foreward; I will not move on.**

At the time, I didn't understand that grief can last forever. Grief flows like a stream in the core of our being. At first, the pain of grief strikes like a tsunami, sudden and unexpected. Thankfully, the torrents of emotion get further and further apart. The pain is always there, but it does subside. It lessens but does not disappear. People asked, "When will you get over this?" That question hit me like a punch to the gut, time and again! You can't simply get over it. In fact, I didn't—and still don't—want to "get over" the loss of my husband. I did want to move past the initial shock and devastation, and I do want to move forward in a productive, positive. and happy manner. However, I will never get over it. That is imposed.

I will move forward; I will not move on.

LIFE AS A WIDOW

I'm sorry to hear that your husband travels a lot for work. But until you know for a fact that he won't ever be home to help you unclog your toilet . . . it's really not the same thing.

—*Catherine Tidd,*
Confessions of a Mediocre Widow

Life as a widow and as a widowed parent has been difficult. It has meant making decisions alone, questioning whether I was doing the right thing, wondering whether I was giving my kids too much in order to compensate for the loss of their dad, and figuring out how to do things I never had to do before—like unclog the toilet!

I was a widow. A widow at thirty-nine! I thought becoming a widow happened later in life. What did this mean? What was I supposed to do? I had no friends who were widows; I had no one to relate to. My friends were either married or divorced. They couldn't begin to understand how painful it was for me to hear of their wedding anniversaries or weekend getaways, or to hear their complaints about their ex-husbands. Living as a widow is just as confusing, difficult, and painful as the initial loss; it's living with a profound feeling of being truly alone. If only Rob had known that living without him is so much harder than living with him and his illness!

I often wondered about what would have, could have, or should have been. What would have been different if Rob were still around? Imagine for yourself that a member of the family is gone from every memory and event over the past five months. How about five years? Fifteen years? How would that change you? How would it have changed the past? What would be different if that person were not around?

Survivors do not receive a road map for the future at the casket of the departed.

I unexpectedly found myself excluded from couples' events. I was no longer part of a group. I was single again. A widowed single with three children. The social isolation was real and created a fresh kind of pain.

> *Survivors do not receive a road map for the future at the casket of the departed.*

Many people seemed to falsely assume that—because I managed to get up, take a shower, dress, and make an appearance at the grocery store—I was doing great. The appearances of grief can be deceiving.

I lied, many times. For a while, I didn't have it in me to tell people my husband died by suicide. I was so confused and afraid that they would judge Rob or me. I told people he had cancer, as that was so much easier; people *support* others with cancer and *judge* those who die by suicide. I avoided people so that I wouldn't have to worry about sharing something that I didn't understand, something that was so painful.

My plate overflowed with duties and responsibilities. I worried and lost sleep, a vicious cycle. At times, depression took over. The pressure and worry led to resentment as I watched everyone around me living "normal" lives.

I worried about my kids constantly: Am I doing enough? Am I doing too much? How do I compensate for Rob's loss? How will I ever know if I've done enough to help them get through and, quite honestly, survive? Being the only parent responsible for them, watching their pain and struggles, and searching for a source of relief was overwhelming.

The kids struggled. I worried that Rob's struggles would also consume them. I worried about their personal pain: broken hearts, lost jobs, bullies, feelings of inadequacy. The worry never stops. I worry about their children and their children's children. I ask the question all the time—will history repeat itself?

I began to look for signs of illness in my children. I witnessed defiant behavior, anger, grief, self-medication, depression, anxiety, alcohol abuse, and an eating disorder in my own children.

I began to worry more. I worried every day about everything. I worried that depression would take control of one of my kids.

I was so alone.

QUESTIONS

Ask me no questions, and I'll tell you no fibs.

—Oliver Goldsmith,
She Stoops to Conquer

People mean well, most of the time. Yet comments full of good intentions can stun and wound. Why would a person ask a grieving mother these questions:

"Why would your husband do this to you and your kids?"
"How did he do it?"
"Is this the first time he tried to kill himself?"

Or plainly state:

"At least it's not a divorce. A divorce is so much harder."
"I lost my mom this year. She was eighty-five and passed in her sleep. I know how you feel."

Friends, family, and people whom I didn't even know asked me these questions. Ignorant people say and ask ignorant things. I began to realize they hadn't been through what I had. They hadn't experienced this type of loss; therefore, they certainly couldn't understand it. I began to let those comments go; I wouldn't wish a loss like mine upon anyone just for the sake of understanding.

I experienced what I call turtle syndrome. I slowly peeked my head out and looked around. I moved slowly back into the real world. I didn't want people to see me when I went out. I definitely couldn't engage in conversations that would make me smile or laugh. What did I have to laugh or smile about? Worse was when I saw people point; I knew that they were talking about me and my situation. When I heard people whisper, "Her husband is the one who killed himself," my heart broke even more. It forced me back into the turtle shell.

I experienced what I call turtle syndrome.

Over time, people changed. Their responses changed. Some family members who would come around soon stopped. Friends who were our friends as a couple were no longer close. Business relationships ended. Why? Was it too hard to be around me and the kids without Rob? Did they blame me? The lost relationships stung. It was fresh pain. I never imagined being forced to live this new life with so many changes and so much loss, disappointment, and grief.

TRITE WORDS

They say everything happens for a reason. Sometimes it would be nice to know that reason.

—Author unknown

After the loss of Rob, people—friends and strangers alike—often said to me, "Everything happens for a reason."

I refused to agree.

In fact, I would become frustrated with anyone who would utter those trite words. How selfish, I thought. How flippant, I thought. I felt they were being insensitive and pushing aside the pain. I didn't get it. What were they talking about? What reason could there possibly be? I saw no silver lining amid the storm clouds of grief.

Why do I have to watch my kids grow up without their dad?

In my mind, I fired back question after question: Reason, you say? What reason? Why do I have to watch my kids grow up without their dad? Why did he die in that way? Why did he suffer so much? What reason could there possibly be?

LOSS OF A SPOUSE

Nothing can bring you peace but yourself.

—*Ralph Waldo Emerson*

My husband was gone and was never coming back.

Of all the questions that I was asked, one caught me completely off guard: Would divorce have been easier?

About a month after Rob died, a friend found out her husband was having an affair. She came over with another friend, and they told me all about her husband's cheating. She was understandably devastated, but then she asked the question.

"Vonnie, which do you think is easier to handle? Death or divorce?"

I was shocked. I was irritated. I was confused. I was, admittedly, at a complete loss for an answer. I wanted to respond, "How can you compare the two?"

Both death and divorce are undoubtedly painful. Both involve the loss of a dream. Both result in the loss of family. Holidays are different; birthdays and graduations will never be the same.

Death is death. Loved ones do not return.

But with death, we are reminded every day that a spouse is gone. Forever. They are no longer here.

Death is death. Loved ones do not return.

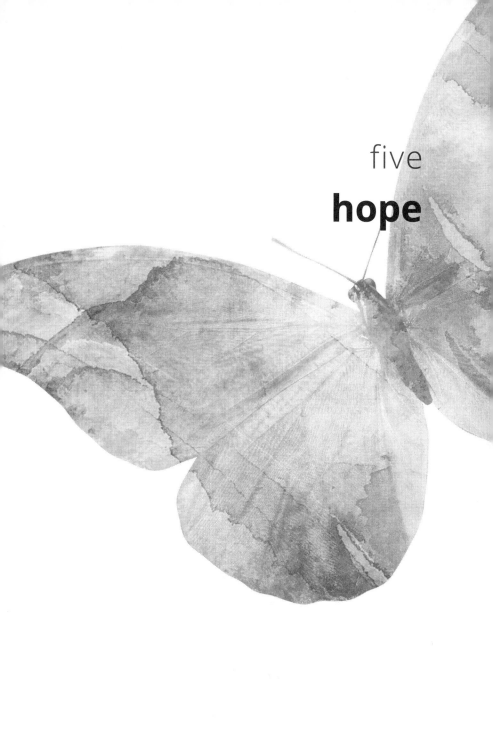

five

hope

BALLOON

Hope is being able to see that there is light despite all of the darkness.

—*Archbishop Desmond Tutu*

The journey of grief was long and often lonely. There were no quick fixes or overnight transformations. It took time. Along the way, there were signs of hope, serendipitous moments that changed me. Often, people focus on big moments (e.g., anniversary dates) or significant changes (e.g., relocating) in the grieving process. But I found the silver lining of hope in the smallest of things—everyday occurrences that took on new and unexpected meaning in the wake of Rob's death.

The day he died, I decided to take a walk. It was a dark and dreary Michigan day. My mind was so jumbled. At times, it felt like the walls were closing in on me. I needed to get out. I needed to clear my head.

As I looked out the window to check on the weather, I was surprised. A hot-air balloon was floating in the cloudy sky! I just stared at it, wondering if my imagination was playing a trick on me. But I wasn't dreaming; the balloon was there. Whitney yelled out from her bedroom that there was a balloon in the sky. There really was a red balloon in the sky! But why? That didn't make any sense; it wasn't the right time of year for a balloon ride.

At that moment, I recalled the blanket and my words to Rob in the hospital: "I've covered you with a blanket with hot-air balloons.

That is something we have never done. When you get better, we'll go for a hot-air balloon ride." Seeing the balloon in the sky and the memory of that moment with Rob gave me chills and brought tears to my eyes. I believe it was a sign from Rob. He wanted me to know he was OK. I had always believed in signs, and that moment assured me; I had received one from above.

The balloon was the first of many signs that would follow.

This would be the first sign from Rob, a sign that he was OK now and that he was no longer suffering: a red hot-air balloon sailed through the cold Michigan air. The balloon was the first of many signs that would follow.

SKIS

Happy times come and go, but the memories stay forever.

—Author unknown

A few months after Rob's death, we returned to our cottage in northern Michigan on what would have been Rob's birthday weekend. The kids and I went to the place that Rob loved so much. We needed to remember and celebrate him there. The snowy February weather was perfect for one of his favorite activities: skiing.

The grief and pain of losing Rob was still fresh, visceral, and all too real. He was gone. Tears and memories followed one after the other like the beats of a drum that weekend.

Close friends who lived nearby and had come to Rob's funeral were a tremendous support that weekend. We lacked nothing.

Stepping outside into the cold air, I felt the crisp winter chill in my lungs. The sun was glistening on the snow. I thought of how much Rob would have loved this.

The memories of him—the good memories— remained.

We made many, many memories that weekend, but one moment has stood out for me. I vividly recall helping the kids put on their gear: coats, boots, skis, and gloves. Memories of Rob flooded my mind. I remembered how Rob put on his gear and helped the kids with theirs. Everything seemed so very familiar, yet one person was missing—Rob.

i understand

As I looked out at the beautiful pine trees, though, I remembered Rob's pine casket with skis engraved on the side. A coincidence? Maybe. But I didn't think so then, and I don't think so now.

I did not see Rob that day. There were no shadows or whispers. But I felt the wind—as it shook the snow from pine needles—and knew he was there, present with us. The memories of him—the good memories—remained. They stayed with us as part of us. I felt a moment of comfort and saw a ray of light in the darkness of grief. It was a sign of hope.

LAUGHTER

Sometimes crying or laughing are the only options left, and laughing feels better right now.

—*Veronica Roth,* Divergent

After Rob's death, days passed in muted sadness. The absence of joy created a curious silence—a deafening stillness, a world without smiles and joy. Amid the chaos that followed Rob's death, I don't recall being aware that the laughter had stopped. I realized its absence when it returned.

Seven months after Rob died, I heard myself laugh. That strange and wonderful sound! Something so simple, so natural, and so human.

It was a silly moment. A simple moment. An unexpected moment of humor.

A friend was helping me with a boat lift, and we had trouble connecting the boat. My friend needed to go under the water, so he asked for a diving mask. I offered my daughter's mask. The friend took a deep breath and submerged. He burst out of the water a few seconds later, looking ridiculous. A grown man wearing a child's mask! Needless to say, it was far too small; and the pink color, although comical, did not match the diver.

The return of laughter was part of my return to life.

My laughter was pure. It came with no effort—freely and unyielding. The laughter echoed through the air. It felt good. I felt alive. I laughed! I was alive.

The return of laughter was part of my return to life. The sentence of silence that followed Rob's death had begun to lift. A simple note of laughter. Another sign.

INCREDIBLE HULK

Actually, I just woke up one day and decided I didn't want to feel like that anymore, or ever again. So, I changed, just like that.

—*MariaLisa deMora,*
Cassie, *Book Twelve*

A few months before Rob died in 2003, I celebrated my birthday with him, our kids, and some friends. It was a low-key celebration at our cottage. We all went to Boyne City for dinner at my favorite northern Michigan restaurant, Red Mesa Grill.

As we headed back, Rob said he needed to run into the supermarket, so I continued home while he went there. Once we were all back at the cottage, we cut into the cake Rob picked up during his stop. While opening gifts, Rob handed me a plastic grocery bag and said, "This reminded me of you." I peeked inside, and then, with a confused smile, I pulled out an Incredible Hulk stuffed figure. I first thought that he must have forgotten a gift and grabbed something at the grocery store while picking up the cake. But I also remembered that collecting superhero figures and comic books was one of Rob and Chase's favorite shared activities. Rob enjoyed collecting Iron Man; Chase loved Batman. I quickly concluded that this was Rob's attempt to include me in their world of superheroes.

The Incredible Hulk doll was the last material gift I received from Rob.

Years later, a friend who saw Rob give me the Hulk brought it up. "Vonnie, I think about the gift Rob gave to you on your birthday often. Do you understand the message in that gift?" I looked at her, a bit perplexed; that night seemed so long ago. She went on to explain: "The Incredible Hulk has the power of super strength and enhanced healing abilities. Rob knew and wanted you to be reminded of your strength and knew you would heal yourself and the kids too."

That comment really made me think. I still wonder about that gift. Did Rob know then? Could it be? Could that really be true? Was that Rob's mindset? Again, it makes me question if he knew his fate months before it happened. Was that his way of offering me hope and strength? It has taken a long time to heal, and quite honestly, I will be healing for the rest of my life. Yet I have found encouragement through this unexpected and untraditional gift of the Incredible Hulk. This unexpected gift is a powerful symbol.

JUNIOR MINTS

My daddy said that the first time you fall in love it changes you
forever, and no matter how hard you try, that feeling just never
goes away.

—*The Notebook*

Six months after Rob died, I joined friends to watch a new movie,
The Notebook. It was the summer of 2004. We surveyed the array of
choices at the concession stand—candy, soft drinks, pretzels, and
popcorn! That moment of decision always reminded me of Rob. We
watched so many movies together and stepped up to countless count-
ers to place our orders. Rob always considered all the options and
then made the same choice.

On that summer day, my good friend pur-
chased a large box of Junior Mints for us to share
and said, "You can't watch a movie without Junior Mints!" I stopped. I stared. I think my jaw
hit the floor.

Gone but not forgotten.

Those were Rob's words. Junior Mints were his
candy. In twenty years of knowing him, I never knew Rob to watch
a movie at the theater without Junior Mints. The Junior Mints in
the dark theater were shadows of him, of us, and of our shared life
together. Gone but not forgotten.

As the movie played, I wanted to break down and cry. I took
the mints as another sign. Life would go on, but memories of Rob
would remain.

EAGLE

Love cures people—both the ones who give it and the ones who receive it.

—*Karl Menninger*

When Rob had been gone for a year, I was with the kids at the cottage in northern Michigan. So many memories were there.

The beginning of a new year, 2005, was just around the corner. I had hoped to take the girls skiing that day, but the snow that was there days earlier had already melted.

Since the weather was unexpectedly warm, I decided to take a walk. As I went, I stopped to enjoy the beautiful view of the lake, with its ice melting under the sun and the water glistening as if stars fell from the sky onto the lake. I again realized why this was one of Rob's favorite places.

I reflected on our first year without Rob. A massive hole gaped in my heart. The daily sadness had not dissipated. As I walked, confusion, my constant companion, returned. The same—now old—questions also returned: Why did Rob leave us? Why must we struggle daily with our loss? Why must my children live without their father?

I spoke one of my favorite quotations out loud: "We must let go of the life we dreamed of and accept and love the life we are given."

The quotation—nineteen simple words—is easy to understand and easy to imagine. Actually living it? That is another matter.

I was looking for answers. A signal. A sign. Anything!

I saw a bird approaching at a distance, and tears started flowing from my eyes when I realized it was an eagle—a favorite of Rob's. Eagles also have significant meaning for me. They represent the past, the present, and the future. I stopped and watched for three or four minutes, wishing someone could come see it with me. Was I dreaming? Hallucinating? My gaze followed the eagle as it faded away in the distance.

I was looking for answers. A signal. A sign. Anything!

I ran to a friend's cottage with tears in my eyes and told her what I saw. She knew of Rob's connection to eagles. She held me as I wept. Then she smiled and said, "Vonnie, Rob did an awful and terrible thing to you, but he keeps coming back to send you messages and guide you." I thanked her for the words of wisdom.

On this last day of 2004, I received a message of hope.

HEMINGWAY

Let it find you. Serendipity, the effect by which one accidentally stumbles upon something truly wonderful, especially while looking for something entirely unrelated.

—Author unknown

Our family spent vacations and holidays in and around Horton Bay, Michigan. That area had been an inspiration for Ernest Hemingway's short stories about the fictional Nick Adams. People wonder about the relationship between Hemingway and Adams. Were they one and the same?

In one poignant moment near the end of *The End of Something*, Hemingway writes:

> Nick said nothing. The liquor had all died out of him and left him alone. Bill wasn't there. He wasn't sitting in front of the fire or going fishing tomorrow with Bill and his dad or anything. He wasn't drunk. It was all gone. All he knew was that he had once had Marjorie and that he had lost her. She was gone and he had sent her away. That was all that mattered. He might never see her again. Probably he never would. It was all gone, finished.

Given the outcome of Hemingway's life—death from suicide—some wonder whether Adams here was a stand-in for Hemingway's own emotions and feelings. Was Adams a written mirror of Hemingway?

Rob long had an interest in Hemingway, both his life and his writing. Like Hemingway, Rob had a deep fondness for Horton Bay. Hemingway's writings gripped Rob. In the wake of Rob's death, I began to wonder if there were more bonds between Rob and Hemingway. Did Rob in some way identify with Hemingway and his struggles?

Rob shared his passion for Hemingway with me and our children. Chase in particular continued his father's fascination. He wanted to know more about Hemingway. Chase read books by and about Hemingway. He would talk for hours with a family friend who was also a Hemingway aficionado.

The girls, too, developed a keen interest in this writer. They began to see resemblances between their dad and Hemingway: their love of Key West, their passion for fly-fishing, and their suicides. Whitney watched a documentary by Mariel Hemingway, *Running from Crazy*. Immediately after watching it, she called and asked me whether I had seen it. I had not. I promised her that I would.

Years later, the girls and I read Mariel's memoir, *Out Came the Sun: Overcoming the Legacy of Mental Illness, Addiction, and Suicide in My Family*. After reading this book and serendipitously meeting Mariel, Maddie said, "I've never felt this emotional while reading a book. From the first chapter of Mariel's book, I see scary similarities between me and her, her family and ours. It's so strange. It's like I am reading about myself." Mariel was able to talk to Maddie, and for the first time Maddie felt as if there was someone who could relate to her and her own family dynamics.

There was life after Ernest; there would be life after Rob.

i understand

Rob's connection to Ernest and our connection to the Hemingway family offered hope. Some people call it serendipity, coincidence, or a "God wink." Whatever the name and whatever the cause, healing and hope have emerged from the intersection of our lives.

There was life after Ernest; there would be life after Rob.

TARA

I am very competitive, so when I fail I use what I learned from
that mishap to fuel success.

—Tara Lipinski

Years before Rob's death, he and I met Tara Lipinski—an Olym-
pic gold medalist in figure skating—through a strange set of
circumstances.

Over the years we stayed in touch.

Several weeks after Rob died, I was in bed late one evening. My
phone rang, I answered, and it was Tara on the other end. She said
something like, "Vonnie, it's Tara. I'm so sorry to hear about Rob.
I haven't been home in weeks, and I just read your letter." Her kind
call was unexpected. We talked openly and frankly about what happened to Rob. She listened and understood. I shared with her that
the night before he died, Rob promised me that nothing would happen to separate him from me and our children.

She then shared her own story of battling depression. She told
me her mom was her cheerleader, providing constant love and encouragement. Her mom would talk to her and get her through the
night. But in the morning—her worst time of day—she had to start
the battle with depression all over again. In Tara's words, "The moment changed." The morning was different. Her words provided
clarity about something that was bothering me. I had long wondered
why Rob would tell me he wouldn't do "that" to his family and then
wake up the next day and do "that" very thing. How could someone

change so quickly, from one day to the next? I now knew; the moment changed for him, as it does for so many people who struggle with suicide.

Tara's words quickly became my own. When people ask me the very question that I asked Tara, I give her response. "The moment changed. Your loved one was fighting an internal battle. In that moment, they felt they needed to end it all." Three simple words—"the moment changed"—changed me. They changed how I understood Rob and what happened.

I was beginning to understand.

Tara's words were yet another sign, a beacon of insight. I was beginning to understand.

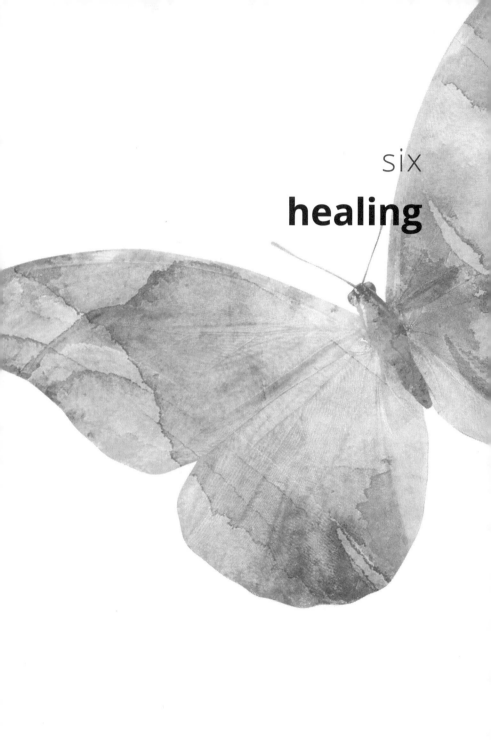

six

healing

GOOD FROM BAD

I have always believed, and I still believe that whatever good or bad fortune may come our way we can always give it meaning and transform it into something of value.

—*Hermann Hesse*

My heart and my mind were slowly healing. Yet questions continued to haunt me. Why did this happen? Why must we suffer so? Can any good come from this?

One night I had a television show on, and I heard the word "widow." I stopped to listen. It was a documentary about a man who had died of cancer. A minister was interviewing his wife. At one point, he asked her, "What good has come out of your husband's death?"

The widow sat in silence, unable to answer. I thought, "What kind of question is that? How dare he ask her such a thing."

He repeated the question several times. Each time the widow's expression looked like disbelief. Then he asked her, "Is your family closer?"

"Oh, yes," she replied. "We have become much closer as a family since the illness and my husband's death."

"That is a good thing, isn't it?" he said.

I thought about what he was trying to accomplish with the questions. I wondered if I would even allow myself to find the good in death. Rob's passing was so difficult for us, the loss so great. Could I look for the good in something that was so awful? The question consumed me. What good has come out of Rob's death? Did I have the courage to admit to good? Was I unfair or disrespectful toward Rob if I could genuinely admit something good had come from his death?

It's difficult to answer because we loved him so much. We would never trade him or his life for something good to come out of it; we would rather have him with us.

What good has come out of your husband's death?

I started to see the courage that I was given because of Rob's death. I was able to speak up about suicide and not let my life be defined by his death or his illness. I learned to be proud of who I am and who he was.

I believe that the moment we dare to admit that good things can come out of the bad—even death—is when we truly begin to heal and find our path. It is then that we can open our hearts to love again.

HEARTBREAK

My heart broke, literally, about ten years after Rob died. I went to the emergency room because I felt like an elephant was sitting on my chest. The doctors immediately admitted me into Metro Hospital. I was having a heart attack.

The next day they took me to surgery to place a stent in the hopes of avoiding future blockage. I was put on the operating table and shown an animated book that explained the procedure. I fell asleep anticipating that I would wake with the stent. But that didn't happen. My doctor informed me that my arteries were clean; there was no blockage. That's when doctors told me that I suffered from cardiomyopathy, also known as broken heart syndrome. My heart literally broke from the continued trauma and stress of life after Rob's death.

I began the road to recovery, the journey to understanding.

The doctor told me, "I don't know what you have going on in your life, but you need to change it." This was a wake-up call for me. I began asking myself, Why don't I accept more help? Why don't I take more breaks? Why don't I respect myself enough to prevent people from taking advantage of me? Why do I surround myself with broken people whom I think I can fix? Was I trying to fix them because I couldn't fix Rob? I asked myself a lot of questions and decided to change my life.

So I changed. I began the road to recovery, the journey to understanding. I started standing up for what I believe. I claimed the courage to say goodbye to toxic people and make my own needs a priority. I began to understand the power of love to heal and offer hope.

JOURNALING

Journal writing, when it becomes a ritual for transformation, is
not only life-changing but life-expanding.

—*Jennifer Williamson*

After losing Rob, I thought I was also losing my mind. My thoughts
raced constantly. Anxiety, fear, doubt, and confusion became constant companions. Intrusive ideas clouded my brain. My mind was a
scrambled mess. I couldn't think straight. My memory was poor.

Even the smallest tasks—like preparing mac and cheese or a
peanut butter and jelly sandwich—seemed too difficult. I simply
couldn't do them; I did not know where to begin. For weeks and
weeks, I went through the motions. Friends recognized my disori-
entation and helped. I would not have made it through the days,
weeks, and months after Rob's death without them chipping in.
Family helped, too. My mom was a busy bee preparing food, doing
laundry, and transporting the kids.

I had to find myself again. Amid the chaos and confusion that
had taken over my life, I had to find me. I had to figure out how to
organize my mind, categorize my thoughts, and regain some sense
of control.

So, I began to journal.

I started with legal pads. I turned to actual paper so I could sit
on my bed at night while the kids slept and get all my day's thoughts
onto something real. I always used the same kind of pen, one that
I found fit my hand and would slide across the paper with ease.

i understand

I started slowly. My first entry was the letter at the start of this book. That letter signaled the beginning of a journey to capture my thoughts and reclaim myself with the real hope of moving forward. Putting my thoughts in writing, especially in letter form, helped me. I don't know why. I can't fully explain it. Things came together, and there was a real sense of relief. I could express my experiences, my fears, and my truths after our loss. The page does not gossip, distort, twist, or mock. It does not judge or condemn. The page accepts. It listens and stores. You give and it receives. Every letter, every word, and every sentence was a catharsis.

Days turned into weeks; weeks into months. I journaled and journaled and journaled. I recorded the first time I laughed after losing Rob. I wrote down the memories of Rob shared by others. All on the page.

As I write now, I have been journaling for fifteen years. The pages are the record of my life.

Writing those memories, those echoes of the past, saved me then and remind me now of what was. It is strange how much I have forgotten, small things and big things alike. The stress and trauma of Rob's loss left blank holes in my mind. My nephew, not long ago, was telling me a story about Rob. He started talking about a black Corvette, and I gave him a confused look. He said, "You don't remember the Corvette, do you?" I didn't. How had I forgotten? How can anyone fail to recall their spouse's dream car? I tried so hard to remember something—anything!—but nothing came to me. My head felt full, as if it would explode from my futile attempt to remember. To this day, I try so hard to recall that car. I can't remember it, but it is in my journal! The memory lives in the minds of others and on the pages of my journal.

As I look back now over the years, I can see the hills and valleys of my journey. I have come a long way. I shed many tears over the pages. The emotions and feelings poured out of me along with the words.

I am amazed now, when looking over the pages, that I seemed to end my entries consistently with something positive. That is curious, even to me. In the beginning stages of journaling, I found peace in what we still had. Memories of our family were precious, and they couldn't be taken away. Journaling saved those memories. From my journal, I have this book.

Penmanship changes and paper wrinkles. The conversations created through the written word endure.

I love quotations. I connect with them and understand myself better in the words of others. I started adding meaningful quotations in the pages of my journal. My words and those of others flowed together on the pages. I was not alone. Others, too, had walked similar journeys, felt similar pain, and wrestled with similar doubts. Our lives, like the words on the page, mingled together, across time and place.

Since my journaling began, my style has evolved. My feelings are now more descriptive. I now use the computer to journal, as corrections are much easier to make. I have even entered all my handwritten journaling pages into the computer.

Penmanship changes and paper wrinkles. The conversations created through the written word endure. Journaling changed my life.

TIME FOR CHANGE

Life is about trusting your feelings, taking chances, finding happiness, learning from the past and realizing everything changes.

—Author unknown

On my fiftieth birthday, I decided to make a change.

In the past, birthdays were marked by frivolity and celebration: special dinners, champagne, and gifts! However, on that milestone birthday, the reality of my life hit me hard. I was tired of feeling alone in a crowd of people. Those around me—although kind, loving, and supportive—were not like me. I didn't have friends who understood what it was like to live without a spouse and in the shadow of a loss from suicide. I simply couldn't look at that day, my birthday, as I had in the past. Too much had changed.

On that day, I looked back on the previous ten years. The journey from December 2003, the month of Rob's death, to July 2014 was long, complicated, and scary. In that time, I questioned everything. Myself. Rob. Life. There were so many questions and so few answers.

The path was marked by pain, devastation, loss, illness, abuse, depression, and anxiety.

Life was now different.

As I reflected on those years of struggle, I recalled some moments vividly. Other moments seemed but a fog. I couldn't help but be thankful to have survived the wake of Rob's suicide. I remembered the countless faces and names of people

I met along the way—friends and strangers, individuals on their own journeys. Suicide touches many lives and casts a long shadow.

Life was now different. I thought about it differently. I was beginning to understand.

A REASON

With everything that has happened to you, you can either feel
sorry for yourself or treat what has happened as a gift. Everything is either an opportunity to grow or an obstacle to keep you
from growing. You get to choose.

—Author unknown

My husband's death made me a better parent, it made me more
accepting of others, and it taught me not to judge. Death was the
teacher; I was the student. Rob's death brought new people into my
life. I learned more about suicide and mental health. The struggles,
the hurdles, the agony, and the pain trained me. Grief prepared me
for something new.

I accepted that Rob was never coming back. I also accepted that
something good could come from something bad.

I stopped looking for others to make me happy. I found content-
ment within myself. I found so much gratitude for everything that
I still had.

I realized that I could help others with their own losses and tragedies. I found a reason, a purpose, from Rob's death. Did he die so
I could help others live? Did I learn about unconditional love so I
could love others rather than judge them?

I'm supposed to be right here where I am. By helping others I
found the light at the end of the tunnel, the silver lining. It is a bittersweet place to be, knowing that I had to lose Rob to make a dif-

ference, to be able to take a dark subject and make it comfortable to talk about.

I started i understand.

I created i understand to generate conversation about suicide. Ignorance thrives in the darkness. I began to share my story. My whole story! The organization made me feel that I was no longer alone. I was able to go from an army of one to an army of thousands. I learned the power and comfort of, "I get it. I know. I understand."

I created i understand to generate conversation about suicide.

It's when we can understand the reason behind and beyond the pain that we truly heal and say, "I understand." We then can see how love heals.

seven

i understand

I UNDERSTAND

People don't always need advice. Sometimes all they really need is a hand to hold, an ear to listen, and a heart to understand them.

—Author unknown

For years after Rob's death, I tried to explain what happened. To myself. To my children. To others. Those seven little letters in one simple word—"suicide"—were hard to overcome.

They carried a stigma, a stain. I wondered if I could have stopped his pain. I tried to explain. I tried to help people understand. In conversations, I would say things like, "Suicide is not what you think it is." People were puzzled and gave me strange looks. My words often failed me.

Sometimes I would lay in bed at night, wondering what it would take to change the conversation. I tossed and turned, grasping for a way to help people understand. Why do people have to suffer in this way? Why can't we be honest with others? Why can't we talk about suicide?

Why do people believe that suicide is a choice, a crime, a sin, or a selfish act?

I finally had enough. Enough of the questions. Enough of the explanations. Enough of the confusion. Enough of the pain. Something had to change.

My experiences with the pain of losing Rob could catalyze that change. First with my own children, then with others. It all begins with conversation, honest dialogue. Silence can lead to loneliness; loneliness to depression; depression to death by mental illness. Silence can be deadly.

I talked with my kids about their and their children's high susceptibility to depression and anxiety. I made them promise that we would always talk. If the dark clouds of depression started to appear, we would talk. We would seek treatment. We would go to appointments. We would seek out friends and family.

It was time to come out of the shadows and challenge the darkness of pain and depression.

But the message goes further. The problem reaches beyond my family. For some reason, we—I mean you as well, reader—assume that mental illnesses are to be hidden, not talked about. We wear masks and muzzles to hide our pain.

In response, my children and I created i understand. It was time to come out of the shadows and challenge the darkness of pain and depression.

We did not know what to expect. There were many questions, both serious and mundane. Would anyone care? How would the medical community respond? Would others share our beliefs? Who would help? How would they help? What color should our heart symbol be? Would anyone want to wear a T-shirt simply to provoke a conversation?

Created in 2014, i understand is a nonprofit organization with a set of core beliefs:

i understand suicide is an effect of an illness
i understand mental illnesses/brain illnesses are treatable
i understand stigma is the primary reason why someone would
    not seek treatment for mental illness; education and awareness
    are vital to saving and changing lives

i understand reaching out to those who are suffering could save a
    life; let someone know you are available and treat them with
    respect and compassion
i understand most people who are suicidal do not want to die;
    they want their pain to end
i understand speaking out about suicide may empower others to
    share their stories
i understand feelings of guilt are part of the grieving process on
    the way to finding peace and acceptance
i understand those who die by suicide do make it to heaven

Our goals were simple and threefold. First, create a community of support, love, and understanding. Second, create awareness about suicide and mental health issues. Third, help others feel less alone.

For those who have been touched by mental illness or of the loss of a loved one to suicide, we offer compassionate comfort. We want to ensure that those who have fallen victim to the pain of mental illnesses are remembered.

For others, we seek to educate. We want everyone to understand.

We started small. Whitney designed a logo that communicates a simple but profound message: a simple pink heart. Pink, the color of unconditional love, reminds us to love ourselves enough to get the help we need and to love others for who they are. Pink is our signature color, constantly reminding us to love unconditionally.

We then took small steps forward, focusing on people who had lost someone to suicide. We formed a local community. Together, we laughed, cried, and vented. We were safe with each other. Safe from the stares, comments, and questions. Our stories were different yet identical. We bonded through shared experience. Our lives are different from what we thought or planned. We walk together one day at a time. Moment to moment. Day to day. Week to week. Month to month. Year to year.

i understand

Internally, we formed a real community—bound by pain, determined by love. The outpouring of kindness and support was amazing. In our little group, the shattered pieces of lives started to come back together. Help. Healing. Wholeness.

Externally, we are changing the conversation. We are focusing the dialogue on *why* people die by suicide, not *how* people die. People reach out to us from near and far. We are growing by the day.

Through conversation and education, real change can happen.

SYMBOLS

I don't think people understand how stressful it is to explain what's going on in your head when you don't even understand it yourself.

—Author unknown

Our symbols matter. They communicate deep truths that go beyond words.

The Pink Heart

The pink heart represents the importance of unconditional love. We must love ourselves enough to recognize the help we may need. We must understand the importance of who we are, and we must accept our journey and ourselves along the way. Let's love others unconditionally by accepting who they are and their struggles. The pink heart symbolizes our commitment to providing unconditional love and understanding. Love and understanding heal. Anger and judgment hurt.

The Butterfly

The butterfly symbolizes that change can be beautiful. A caterpillar sheds the old to become something new, a butterfly. This symbol serves as a constant reminder to be strong despite the transitions in our lives.

i understand

Change is inevitable. Tomorrow will be different from today. The butterfly embraces the change. We too embrace the change, being in a dark place yet knowing that we have the ability to emerge into something beautiful.

"The Door Is Always Open"

In 2017, i understand adopted a new symbol—a work of art created by Daniel Carlson for ArtPrize, an annual event that transforms the city of Grand Rapids into an art festival. The event attracts hundreds of artists and thousands of spectators. *The Door Is Always Open* is a larger-than-life work of art in copper and steel (http://www.artprize .org/66344). It stands more than fifteen feet high and depicts a cage, a man, and a butterfly. Imagine a giant bird cage with a man standing inside. The figure of the man is composed of circular pieces of steel, a metal that is tough but deteriorating. The man, seemingly immovable and trapped by his fierce hold on the bars, is unaware of the open door behind him. *The Door Is Always Open* perfectly captures the message of i understand. It offers a visual that evokes a question: "What does this man in the cage represent?"

The Cage with an Open Door

Why the open door? Even though we know help is available, we struggle to act when situations are hard or when things are difficult to discuss. The door is open, but we don't walk through.

Why are we afraid of the outside? Do we fear the unknown, the judgment of others, or perhaps the denial within us? Each of these fears can explain the behavior of people in the cage. Then it's up to those of us outside the cage to recognize the pain of the person inside the cage, to walk in, and to offer the help that is needed.

The Man

The man stands with his back to the open door and his hands clenched on the bars. He is crumbling before our eyes. It's a symbol of feeling trapped within a struggle with depression, anxiety, addiction, or an unhealthy relationship.

It takes strength and courage to recognize suffering, talk to someone, and seek help.

The man in *The Door Is Always Open* is alone. No other people occupy the cage with him. He has not sought help. As a result, he is struggling inside. The internal battle is inflicting a heavy toll on his body. In the work of art, each circle represents a part of who he is. He is slowly losing himself, deteriorating. The man inside the cage vividly portrays someone in the throes of depression, the plight of over 90 percent of suicide victims.

> *Our symbols matter. They communicate deep truths that go beyond words.*

The man dwells in his own nightmare, failing to seek and then receive the help and support he so desperately needs. You look at his feet and see his deterioration, no longer having the strength to walk out the door alone.

It takes courage—amid the darkness—to turn, face fears, and walk through the open door. The man in the piece wastes away. Others do not have to.

Outside the Cage

The butterfly outside the cage represents freedom from the debilitation of depression. The outside of the cage is scary, as those inside fear judgment associated with mental illness/brain illness. We need to create a place of love without judgment or expectation. In this way, i understand works to help people recognize others who are trapped in their own cages. Looks can often be deceiving. People in cages of mental distress walk past each of us every single day. We only know when we ask, Are you OK? Do you need help?

Those watching someone deteriorate cannot be simply like the passersby near the sculpture. They need to muster the courage to walk through the door and offer help. Love heals.

THINGS WE DO

Wear

It's simple, it's easy, and it's free. It all began with the Wear, Care, Share Campaign.

One of our key goals is to reduce the stress and stigma of talking openly about mental health. The challenge: How do you get people to be vulnerable about their depression, anxiety, and fear? How do you convince people to talk about mental health? How do you persuade people to be real? Two simple words: i understand. These words on the front of a T-shirt prompt people to ask, "What do you understand?" Conversations follow. They are marked by candor, honesty, and attention. These interactions are safe zones where people can talk without prejudice or judgment.

Our first order of shirts arrived on the same day actor Robin Williams lost his battle with mental illness: August 11, 2014. His death pushed suicide and suicide prevention into the national spotlight. People wanted to know more about suicide and its causes. Our simple shirts opened doors for understanding.

We are a mobile army creating safe spaces, conversation, and understanding.

The statement (i understand) that spurred the question (What do you understand?) has also spurred a movement. To date, we have distributed more than 16,000 T-shirts across thirty states and to several countries. We are a mobile army creating safe spaces, conversation, and understanding.

The Wear, Care, Share Campaign never stopped. The response has been overwhelming:

> "I love what you guys are doing! Thank you for encouraging talk and support for mental health. I would be proud to wear a shirt!"
>
> "I lost my son to suicide and struggle with addiction and depression. I would love to wear this to invoke conversation."
>
> "I want to get the word out! It is important to love and understand your neighbor because a loving world could save a life."
>
> "When I see tees on someone else around town (and beyond), I realize that we are part of a community. A community that cares about bringing to light things that could easily be stigmatized."
>
> "I would love to wear the shirt to bring awareness and show that it's not something to hide. I know many people who have been ashamed to speak up about mental health!"
>
> "As someone who lost a father to suicide and struggles daily with mental health, I would love to wear a shirt as a way to say, 'I understand, I will listen, and we can support each other the best as we can.'"
>
> "It's a great conversation starter on how to end the stigma."

By sharing, we help others and we help ourselves. Sharing the belief, the mission, and the passion behind i understand offers relief. People's loneliness diminishes. When they realize they are not alone, that their feelings are not choices, and that others care about them, lives change, new friends are made, and most importantly, help is sought.

It's a simple concept: Wear, Care, Share. It is something we can all do that may have a greater impact than what we realize.

Meet

Fear, sadness, and depression thrive in the shadows; they thrive amid isolation.

The i understand organization brings people together, out of the shadows. We are committed to meeting people in public places and in small groups.

We are committed to being present and active in the community.

We began organizing free community events featuring yoga, tai chi, painting classes, walking, and other activities to build a sense of community and let people know they are not alone.

We also began a support group for those who have experienced loss due to suicide. There, we introduce ourselves by saying our name, our loved one's name, and the cause of their death. For example, "I'm Vonnie, and I lost my husband, Rob, to depression." We focus on *why* they died, not *how*. The culprits are common: addiction, bullying, pain, and depression. We teach and learn from each other, reinforcing the basic message that suicide is caused by pain.

We offer a support group to those who live with someone struggling with a mental health illness and offer ways to support them in a nonjudging way, while also recognizing the importance of self-love and self-care.

> *We are committed to being present and active in the community.*

Every September (National Suicide Prevention Month), i understand hosts a celebration dinner. We invite a prominent speaker who is either a mental health advocate or someone touched by suicide. Ginger Zee, the chief meteorologist for ABC News, recently spoke at the dinner. The event raises money to support the mission of i understand. It also increases awareness in the community and celebrates the lives of those lost to suicide.

i understand

We go to everyday places in order to normalize the conversation about mental health. We are proud to have brought the conversation to sporting events, health fairs, schools, businesses, nonprofit organizations, coffee shops, hospitals, and first-responder stations.

Whether at a widows' dinner, a class on anxiety management, or a presentation on workplace suicide prevention, i understand brings people together to educate, inform, and heal.

We meet together to defeat the stigma of talking about mental health and suicide.

Move

Get up, get out, and walk for the health of it.

Devastation, fear, and loss affect each of us in different ways. It is hard to find healthy coping strategies.

Loss affects our minds *and* our bodies. In the wake of Rob's death, I turned to walking. I walked as often as I could to clear my mind and offer therapy to my heart. I would walk after I dropped the kids off at school, before I picked them up, and then again after dinner. The fresh air, the music I listened to, and the moments of reflection all became immensely important to me.

Get up, get out, and walk for the health of it.

My habit has become a group habit. For the sake of health benefits and fellowship, i understand sponsors and organizes weekly walking events. We meet and talk as we walk. We share support and encouragement. We find life and hope together on the trails and around the corners.

Members of i understand participate in 5K walks and runs, celebrating accomplishments with each other.

Heal

Over time we started to dream bigger. We wanted to make an impact in the community.

One of i understand's realized dreams was raising the money to fully fund a clinical nurse specialist specializing in mental health at Helen DeVos Children's Hospital in Grand Rapids. The nurse has been able to train over 11,000 staff members at Spectrum Health. She implemented the Ask Suicide-Screening Questions (ASQ) for pediatric patients. In 2018 alone, 1,100 patients were screened for suicide risk. This means the nursing staff had 1,100 meaningful conversations with children and adolescents about the risk for suicide. With every conversation and every life she touches, the nurse makes a difference in people's lives. She offers them resources and information about organizations—including i understand. Beyond the local hospital, the nurse specialist has presented her work to the Children's Hospital Association and Solutions for Patient Safety. The former consists of over twenty-two children's hospitals across the United States whose mission is to advance children's health care. The small pink heart of i understand beats strong, both near and far.

We wanted to make an impact in the community.

Among the many comments received from participants in the hospital program, one stands out: "I know these questions are uncomfortable to ask children, but we need to help support our children who are struggling, so they do not act on these thoughts."

We are just beginning. It is part of i understand's mission to provide education and offer compassionate comfort to those children.

Could there be a nurse specializing in mental health in every city to ensure those who have had a crisis receive the love and compassion they deserve? Someone who can educate medical staff about the proper conversation? Someone who can help them recognize that an illness is an illness and that no illness should be judged or dismissed? Is it possible to provide care packages with resources and tools to support patients released from hospital care? Could suicide screening be available to anyone who is in pain?

Our latest project with the children's hospital supports youth on the autism spectrum. We are proud to be funding a sensory room for children who are at risk of harming themselves or others, a safe place of comfort and calm.

THINGS WE SAY

Talk

We believe in the power of words. In i understand we communicate with each other with open, honest, and raw words. Words matter, and words change lives. Talking openly with others helps to heal us.

Fear and stigma drive the culture of silence. Many people are afraid to share or listen to others. They pretend mental illness is far removed from them. They lie to themselves and others. Hard truths are swept under the rug. Denial is a deceptively safe place for many.

When we began i understand, we committed ourselves and each other to communication. So we created a video and posted it online. It was a simple explanation of my own loss and journey to understanding.

Not long after we posted the video, I received a message that stated:

"After watching your video, not only have you saved my life, you've saved my family the devastation of losing me. I always thought they would be better off without me. You have made me see, clearly that is not true."

As I read, tears emerged from my eyes. We spoke, and our words challenged the solitude. Words broke the silence; change happened.

Through i understand, others find peace through understanding things that are difficult to understand. They find i understand to be a safe and comforting community for people who can say, "I get it," "I know," or "I understand."

Words break down walls.

Definition

It is hard to talk about mental pain and its consequences. Too often, when people speak of pain they are told to "ignore the pain" or "get over it." These commands are a call for silence. We must talk. We must be there for each other.

Words break down walls.

My hard truth—I have been as guilty as anyone. It took me well over ten years to start talking openly with others. The conversation begins with the very words we use.

Webster's Dictionary defines suicide as "the act or an instance of taking one's own life voluntarily and intentionally." Martyrdom is defined as "the suffering of death on account of adherence to a cause and especially to one's religious faith." The first word, *suicide*, is damnable; the second, *martyrdom*, is praiseworthy. We believe sinners commit suicide and heroes die a martyr's death. These words and the ideas they communicate matter.

Most people who die by suicide have, at some point in their lives, been diagnosed with depression. A depressed person, by definition, has impaired reasoning capacities. Thought is compromised. The situation is even worse when alcohol is involved. Can we honestly say the following: "The depressed alcoholic intentionally killed herself/himself"? We instinctively know something is wrong with that sentence. Depression and alcohol impair rational intention. More truthful: "Depression killed him/her." Like, "Cancer killed him/her."

Mental illness, such as depression or another mood disorder, is the major catalyst for suicide. It's time to highlight the role of illness and change the definition by narrowing the meaning of suicide. A proposed change is written like this:

Suicide (noun):
Suicide is a side effect of pain, the result of mental illness, mood disorder, and/or physical pain.

—https://www.change.org/p
/change-the-definition-of-suicide

Changing the meaning of suicide is key. "Self-death" is a broader term, including some instances of martyrdom and the right to die.

I believe suicide is a result of pain. A person does it with impaired thinking, not voluntarily or intentionally. If you have a mental illness, you are at risk. If you suffer pain, you are at risk. As we suffer from various forms and degrees of mood disorders, we are all at risk.

Recognizing that suicide is a side effect of pain is an important first step. Acknowledging the true source of suicidal thoughts and actions removes stigma and helps save lives.

Pain is the catalyst and enabler of suicidal thoughts and actions. It comes in many forms.

Mental illness and mood disorders can imprison the mind in a seemingly never-ending existence of suffering.

Physical pain wreaks similar misery on bodies and minds. The pain of the body changes people. They become different.

Social pain from bullying is debilitating, destabilizing, and disorienting. Bullying, among its other effects, makes victims question themselves and literally changes their brains. Suicide is the number two cause of death for youths ages ten to thirty-two. These young people do not choose self-death through a rational thought process. Their thinking, like that of an alcoholic, is impaired.

Divorce and dissolution of relationships cause incredible, often unspeakable, pain. The results are fear, uncertainty, and anxiety. As life moves on, the pain does not always abate.

Financial ruin is devastating. It can cause embarrassment and shame. Pain results, and it often lingers.

Compounding factors contribute to the degree and duration of pain. Risks increase exponentially. Depression, addiction, and difficult life experiences heighten risk.

Pain in its various forms triggers thoughts and reactions that change the body and the brain. Awareness of pain in others and in ourselves creates opportunities to provide help and bring about meaningful change.

Words

We are determined to change the definition and change the conversation.

When Kate Spade—an American fashion designer and businesswoman—died in 2018, I was shocked that many national news organizations focused on the end of her life. Why do we need to dwell on how her illness won? Why do we need to focus on that specific moment of her life? That choice of emphasis affects her family and, more broadly, the way we think about what happens.

Rather than focusing on the act, we can focus on the cause: pain. Rather than centering on *what* happened, we should examine *why* it happened. I believe that if we talk about this differently, we can achieve different results.

When someone asks how my husband died, I can respond in different ways:

One option: "He killed himself." But is that really what happened to him? Is that the entire story? Those words might make you think he was crazy or selfish. He was neither.

Alternatively: "He died of depression." These words communicate a complicated story over time. Rather than casting blame, these words raise questions. What are the signs and symptoms of depression? This answer shifts the focus from the act to the illness.

Suicide is a side effect of pain. All illnesses have side effects; suicide happens to be one of those side effects. We can die from many illnesses, whether from the illness itself or from a side effect. We don't believe suicide is the rational or conscious choice of a healthy person.

It's simple: name the cause; identify the pain. "My husband died from depression." When talking about suicide, stop using the word *commit*. No one commits a suicide. It is not a crime. Stop using the word *kill*; it implies a willful and rational action.

> **Suicide is a side effect of pain.**

Rather, we understand. To say "I understand" is to offer someone compassion—a word of hope and assurance that they are not alone.

These changes in our language make the conversation easier and more educational. They allow those who have lost someone to depression to understand that all illnesses have side effects. As with other illnesses, some people live, some people die. Cancer and depression are, in that way, no different. The illness can take over and win. That is a basic truth.

My husband died from depression. His illness won. I was his biggest cheerleader, and because of that I live with no regret. I know I did everything I could have done with the knowledge I had at the time. I believe I kept him alive longer than he would've been without me. I do often wonder, though, whether things would have been different if I knew then what I know now.

Let's talk about it; let's change the definition. Let's take this dark subject and bring light with understanding. Suicide is not a choice, but we can choose how we understand it.

i understand

We need help if we are going to achieve change. We need you. Will you join us in changing the conversation? We can remove the stigma attached to the word suicide and save lives.

LETTER TO ROB

I wanted to spend the rest of my life with you; but instead I am deeply honored you decided to spend the rest of your life with me.

—*Camille Marette*

October 31, 2019

Dear Rob,

Saying goodbye was so difficult. There were so many uncertainties, decisions to make, and challenges to overcome. I did not understand. My heart was shattered.

It's sad to think the kids have now lived more of their life without you than with you. Yet you impact them each day.

You lost your life to a horrible illness. A confusing and completely devastating illness that wasn't easily talked about. Yet we had to go on, often not knowing how we could. There are moments that I will never forget, like the first time I tried to get the kids to make a Father's Day card for their grandpa or when a friend's dad offered to take our daughter to a daddy-daughter dance. They reacted with words: "But he's not my dad." I didn't push but knew all our hearts ached. That ache has stayed with us year after year. New friends still ask about you. They do not know our story.

We have learned not to judge others.

We have learned suicide is a side effect of mental illness.

i understand

I tried providing positive male role models without success. I learned some lessons the hard way.

The kids have become independent and fierce, certainly a by-product of realizing that I couldn't give or do it all. We are survivors making huge strides to ensure the best future for ourselves despite our tragic loss.

My shattered heart understands.

All three kids have sat by my side creating i understand so we could speak openly about mental health issues and suicide. I have watched a sense of relief come over them. Working with i understand has given them an opportunity to heal and help. We were no longer alone as others started opening up and sharing their own stories of loss and grief. Our turning point of understanding was a gift. A true gift.

There are so many things that I could say. We love you more than you could ever know. We understand that LOVE NEVER DIES. For us, our love has become stronger not only for you but for each other. We know you are with us every day, beaming with pride and helping to guide us. Because of you we are now truer to ourselves. We remember you for how you lived. We live understanding each situation from all sides and never forget that love heals, even love from the most unexpected places. We now accept that love, embrace it, and share it. We know that's what you would want us to do.

My shattered heart understands.

Love heals,

Vonnie

A BETTER TOMORROW

Deep into that darkness peering, long I stood there, wondering, fearing, doubting, dreaming dreams no mortal ever dared to dream before.

—*Edgar Allan Poe,* The Raven

In i understand we dream of a different tomorrow.

In our dream, we envision a world where people talk freely about illness and pain. We dream of a place without judgment, where mental pain is understood and acts of self-harm are seen as the byproducts of mental, physical, or emotional pain.

In our dream, there is no stigma from suicide. Rather, we understand pain is the common denominator of all suicides.

In our dream, depression is understood to be like other illnesses. Some illnesses lead to death; some do not. No blame. No pointing fingers. The illness sometimes wins.

> *In our dream, depression is understood to be like other illnesses.*

In our dream, we recognize and help those suffering from bullying, physical harm, financial loss, heartache, and deception. Although different from depression, these pains are real, deep, and sometimes fatal.

Our dream doesn't have to remain a dream.

At i understand, we want to do more than dream. We want to create a better tomorrow in our homes, cities, states, and nations.

i understand

We want to impact communities near and far with i understand's message of hope and love.

The dream will come true. It's happening in Grand Rapids, Michigan. It can happen where you are, too. Will you be a part of the change?

It's simple. Start by changing the conversation in your home, your workplace, and your community.

Ask questions.

Educate others simply by saying, "I understand."

Be the one.

Love heals.

CONNECTING

We are readily available:

- ♥ https://iunderstandloveheals.org/
- ♥ https://www.facebook.com/iunderstandloveheals/
- ♥ Instagram: iunderstand_loveheals
- ♥ i understand
  P. O. Box 822
  Ada, Michigan 49301

FINAL THOUGHT

Deep down you already know the truth; let's face it together.

—*Vonnie Woodrick*

For those who are struggling with suicidal thoughts, this is for you.

For those who have a loved one that is struggling, be the one.

Dear Friend,

There are things I need you to know. Life can be hard, confusing, and unfair. The struggles you're facing are real. You may feel alone and your pain is so deep—you've contemplated ending it all. I'm here to listen, to care, and to support. It takes courage to seek help, find treatment, and face the inner battle you are fighting.

You're worth it. Your pain is temporary.

Be brave and fight.

Your family loves you even when sometimes you think you're not lovable. If you don't believe that—find a friend, teacher, or coworker to confide in. You need to understand the world is better with you than without you. The pain of losing you would run deep. Your death would cause devastating trauma to your loved ones. The guilt of survivors can last a lifetime. Think again.

It takes one person to make a difference. Will you find that one?

i understand

The one you confide in, the one who supports you, the one who unconditionally loves you, the one who understands. Find someone.
You're worth it. Your pain is temporary.
You're loved. You're not alone.

Love heals,

Vonnie

Help is available 24/7
1-800-273-TALK

growing up in the shadow of suicide

IN THEIR OWN WORDS

We share with people who've earned the right to hear our story.

—*Brené Brown*

Talking with my kids now as adults has allowed me to see their strengths, courage, and wisdom. I'm amazed by all three of my children. As a family, we have walked at times together and at times alone through life without Rob.

The children are now grown. They have their own lives. It is such a joy to talk openly and honestly with them. I learn that I did some things right. Other things I now wish I had done differently.

One of my children once told me, "Mom, if you can look at our lives from our point of view, we couldn't have had a better mom. We needed you. You were chosen for us. We are who we are because of your strength."

Those words, spoken with sincerity and from the heart, are generous. I did my best. Widowhood can be a sad and lonely place. Yet I learned long ago that love can come from the most unexpected places. We are never truly alone.

I end this book with the voices of my children, their words on the page. I include them because I want their truths to be known. For those struggling after a suicide, you and your children are not alone.

i understand

For those contemplating suicide, know as you read the words of my children that people need you—really need you.

Chase

> The fact that many people don't recognize or have patience for your illness only makes everything worse.
>
> —*Ian Thomas*

It's hard to believe that I lost my dad sixteen years ago at the mere age of fifteen. It shattered my world and definitely changed my life path. I was devastated, lost, and very confused. Kind of strange to think I've lived more without my dad than with him, as he is still such a part of my life.

You see, my dad was my *best* friend and my strong foundation. I struggled with learning disabilities, muscle weaknesses, and whatever the diagnosis at the moment was—ADHD, learning disabilities, Asperger's, and more. I was in "special ed," psychiatric therapy, and speech therapy during my younger days. It was my dad who never gave up on me, giving me amazing opportunities. He taught me how to ski and scuba dive. He showed me the power of knowledge through reading; because of his encouragement, I developed a deep love for books.

I fell apart after his death. He spent so much of his time encouraging me, teaching me, and loving me in spite of my many challenges. I think now maybe he saw some of himself in me. He too struggled with math and had problems reciting the alphabet. And he fought against anxiety every day.

Today, I wonder how different my life would be with him still in it. Who would I be, as he is so much a part of who I am? Do I struggle at times with that same anxiety?

Do I question what in this life is worth living for? Do I still grieve? The answers are yes and yes. I often wonder where I belong. You can struggle with learning disabilities yet learn to speak fluent Chinese and become an expert in religion. Even with the instincts of a lion and wisdom beyond my years, there is still the mental health part that always gets in the way.

My anxiety is real. It is not something that I chose. I have found meditation to work for me—without it, the anxiety would be debilitating. The workplace is difficult; people are very judgmental. I have sleeve tattoos yet am extremely articulate. People often wonder why I struggle to find jobs. I have found good jobs, but anxiety usually wins.

My anxiety causes me to be very impulsive. The impulsivity led me to just walk out once. For me, there was a reason—imagine a co-worker walking up to you, fifteen years after your dad died, and saying to you, "You know, your dad's in hell for killing himself." If I hadn't walked out at that moment, I would've punched him.

> **We are never truly alone.**

Those are the things that are still said; the pain never goes away.

Do I have happy moments? Of course. I thank my mom for recognizing the need for unconditional love. If I did not have her and that love, along with the determination to fight an illness that has won in several generations on my father's side, I might not be here.

I keep fighting for you, Mom, and for my sisters. For me, I see it as an accomplishment that I know would make my dad proud. We both can't leave Mom in the same way.

So Dad, today and every day I think of you and am reminded of your encouraging words. I miss you, and as Mom says, "Love never dies; it gets stronger." I will continue to fight to find my way to beat this terrible illness that took you away from me too soon. It is because of you that I am who I am. Even though I do not see you, I feel you. Feeling you is better than not having you at all.

i understand

Whitney

> I don't regret the things I have done. I just regret the things I
> didn't do when I had the chance.
>
> —*Author unknown*

The last day of my life with my dad started out like any other day.
I was twelve years old and a typical seventh-grade girl with an enhanced sense of drama and many opinions. I loved to talk. I loved
being the center of attention, and I was focused—well, at least on
things I loved.

I loved my sister, who was five at the time. She would distract
me from things that I should've been doing, like getting ready for
school. We loved playing silly games. One of them we called "rocks
in our heads." I was playing the game with Maddie that morning. You
play by lying down and repeating a chant (I don't even remember the
chant anymore) while touching different spots on your head. For
some reason, this makes you feel like your head is full of rocks and
you can't sit up. Really, try it; it works.

Maddie was lying in bed next to my dad, watching their favorite
TV show—*SpongeBob SquarePants*. Maddie was really obsessed with
SpongeBob, so my dad always made it a point to watch it with her.
While I was "putting rocks" in Maddie's head, my mom was calling
for me because we had to leave for school. I started to run out to the
car when Maddie shouted that I needed to get the rocks out of her
head. So I ran back in and hurried to reverse this little psychological
spell I had put on her, then began to rush out the door.

My dad called to me to come back and give him a goodbye hug.
I yelled through the doorway, "Sorry, Dad, I'm running late! See you
after school for a hug." And I was off.

My brother and I hated riding the bus, and my mom always felt it important that the last thing we heard before walking into the school for a long day was, "I love you; have a great day!"

My grandma picked me up from school on "that day." This wasn't unusual, as my grandma Savela was a big part of our lives and was always around to help. I wondered where my parents were. It was parent-teacher conference time, and I knew I would be able to go to the book fair in the media center while my parents chatted with my teacher.

My grandma told me she didn't know where my mom and dad were and that she didn't think we would make it to the conferences that night. *What??* I was *furious* as this meant I would have to miss the book fair.

All I was told was that my dad was having some tests done and they were taking longer than usual. I can't imagine the emotions my grandma must have been feeling and how she was able to keep it all together, knowing the real reason my parents were not home.

Little did I know that would be the end of my innocence—when I could think the end of the world was missing the book fair.

My dad never came home, and I never got to give him that hug he asked for. The guilt I carried because of that haunted me for years. For a good ten years, I couldn't talk about my dad without crying.

I felt it was my fault; maybe if I had given him that hug he wouldn't have done what he did. I didn't know the history of his anxiety and depression; I didn't know that members of his family in earlier generations had died in the same way. After all, I was only twelve.

When I heard others talking about how a smile or being nice to someone could make them change their mind about suicide, it destroyed me. I was nice. I smiled. I hugged on all other occasions, just not this one day.

My dad knew I loved him, and he knew I was also a typical twelve-year-old running out the door, making my own needs a priority. Hugging my dad wouldn't have changed what happened "that day." If anything, I believe the love my dad and I shared helped keep him going a bit longer.

I've lived a long time without my dad. I wouldn't want anyone to have to do that. It's been a journey of grief, acceptance, and love from so many who have helped us along the way.

The biggest lesson is also my biggest regret: hug and hug tight. We never know what the next hour will bring, let alone the next day. My life changed tragically, and there's a pain that will last forever in my heart. Live a life with no regret; let others know how much you care, even if it's as simple as a hug. You won't regret it.

Maddie

> I've found that growing up means being honest. About what I want. What I need. What I feel. Who I am.
>
> *—Epiphany*

There is one thing I have always struggled with. It's the initial reaction of people when I tell them not only that my father passed away, but also the circumstances that led to his death. I have always dreaded being introduced to new people or my friends' parents because one of the first questions they ask is, "What does your dad do?" I always respond with the same answer: "He passed away when I was young." Then they always ask the inevitable follow-up question, "How?" I have always considered the word *suicide* immensely harsh. It's just a flat-out ugly word. It is definitely not a word that a young girl should be so comfortable with, and others cower in fear of it.

I have never been embarrassed about how my dad passed away, but I have always been frustrated with the negative connotation of his death. I have always been frustrated with the gape in people's mouths when they say, "Oooh, I'm so sorry . . . " Anyone who has experienced losing someone to suicide can relate to this experience because it is quite obvious that the other person has become seriously uncomfortable and has probably even regretted prodding you on such a "horrific" or "traumatizing" experience. I don't blame them; it's uncomfortable for both of us. But it doesn't have to be.

I want people to know that although my dad's death has affected me, it does not define me. I am not saying I am thankful that my dad died. I would do anything for one last fishing trip or one last afternoon spent watching *SpongeBob SquarePants* with him, but I wouldn't be who I am without it. I've had to mature at a very young age, which has been a blessing and a curse. I have a hard time being around my peers who constantly use the terminology "I want to kill myself" or "Kill yourself" over menial matters that include homework or other minor stressors. Sometimes I wish my experience on this subject only went that far, but I'm glad I am not that ignorant in using such phrases so flippantly. I am thankful for how socially aware I have become, despite knowing the extent my father has contributed to that.

I know I have missed out on a lot of opportunities that only growing up with a father can present, but I am a firm believer that it has not detracted from any aspect of my experience growing up. I am a firm believer that the conventional idea of a family is not the only way to have a family. I am constantly in awe of my mom. Her ability to raise me and my siblings the best way she could is in my opinion equal to or better than what two parents are capable of in some circumstances. I don't care that I've never experienced a daddy-daughter dance. But I do care that I have been fortunate enough to be raised by an utterly selfless woman who is constantly putting the needs of not only her children, but countless others before herself.

In 2014, my mom founded i understand, and quite frankly I was frightened at first. I was scared of what my peers at school would think of me and what they would think about my dad with everything being out in the open.

Being an introvert and being someone who often keeps everything inside, this idea was a nightmare. I didn't want people to look at me differently, I didn't want their sympathy, and I didn't want them to remember my dad as the man who killed himself. All my anxiety was washed away one September day—more specifically and ironically, on National Suicide Prevention Day. All of my friends and many others wore i understand shirts to show support not only for me but for my mother's organization and my dad as well.

I was overwhelmed with happiness, and I was surrounded by genuine support and love. These small acts put everything into perspective for me, knowing there are people who truly do understand and empathize and who are eager to help others. I urge you to learn more about i understand's "Wear, Care, Share" campaign and help to raise awareness in your own school, workplace, or community. The more we talk, the more we encourage others to share their own stories and hopefully help others who are living a daily battle with mental illness.

AFTERWORD

I hope this book about understanding depression, mental health, and suicide will inform and motivate readers. Vonnie's message personally touched me—someone who, although seemingly having it all, has been battling depression for a long time.

This disease does not discriminate. It doesn't matter if you are black or white, rich or poor, male or female. The pain it causes affects everyone. Depression can affect anyone.

Fourteen months ago, I made the decision to change my life. It began with a psychiatry appointment. At the time, I was dealing with a lot of health issues and personal challenges. My doctor was going to increase my depression medications. Before doing so, he asked, "Why drink alcohol, a depressant, when you're depressed?" He encouraged me to give the medicine a better chance to work, without alcohol. He asked me to give up red wine and all alcohol for thirty days.

No doctor, therapist, friend, or bartender had ever said I had a drinking problem.

I told my doctor that not having a glass of red wine at night might *add* to my depression. He didn't see the humor in my comment! I wasn't sure I could go thirty days without any alcohol.

Well . . . more than a year later I have still not had any alcohol. I feel better and have saved thousands of empty calories. I made other changes too: I lost nearly seventy pounds. I exercise, enjoy yoga, surround myself with supportive friends, watch my diet, and go to therapy.

Though not always easy—and sometimes very painful—change is often needed.

I feel so much better emotionally, physically, and spiritually. I have done what I could to be a better me. I sometimes feel like my life has been on hold for over a year; yet, I also feel like I may have added years to my life.

My life still may not be where I would like it to be. Yet, thanks to making the changes needed to change myself, I am confident that good things are coming my way.

In the process, I discovered how many people really care, not only about me, but about others as well. We are never really alone. It may feel that way sometimes (or in my case a lot of times). The support of friends, doctors, and therapists helped me make the necessary changes to be a better, stronger me.

Help is always there to support us in navigating the changes we need to make. We don't even have to ask, just be open to accepting the help we most likely know we need, be willing to do the work, and ask for additional support that is available. It is there, for everyone!

The impact that Vonnie's organization, i understand, is having in our community and beyond is profound. Real change is happening. People are talking about mental health and suicide. Lives are being saved. We can all make simple changes that could result in big changes.

I changed; so can you.

Change can be beautiful. Change is beautiful!

Join me, Vonnie, and others in raising awareness about mental health and suicide. Together, we can break down stigmas and bring much-needed conversations to the forefront.

—*Doug Meijer*
Co-Chairman, Meijer Inc.

ACKNOWLEDGMENTS

A team of people—family, friends, volunteers, and even strangers—helped create and continue to sustain i understand. It takes a community.

My parents offer amazing support. Their contributions are incalculable. My mom does anything that needs to be done, including folding T-shirts, stuffing envelopes, counting pink hearts, and making post office runs. You name it, she does it!

My kids—Chase, Whitney, and Maddie—have also been a tremendous help. Chase helps with manual labor. Whitney creates our graphics and helps with social media. Maddie proofreads and helps with topics of conversation. In return, i understand offers them a platform to talk about their dad in a way that is open, healing, and honest. They refer friends to resources available online. Important, life-sustaining conversations result. They have learned that we all have a story and need to be understood. My children have learned to be slow to judge other people as it increases their risk of judgment from others.

I have been fortunate to have the "A Team" as volunteers. They have been by my side from the beginning. We are a family. Our events give us reasons to come together and enjoy each other's company. Kathy, Paul, Sue, Morgan, Erin, Kit, and Sherry, I couldn't do this without you!

Emily Powers joined our small team to provide us with big support as an i understand project coordinator.

141

acknowledgments

Elyse Wild spent countless hours with me on the first edits of this project. I am forever grateful for Elyse and her encouragement through the process.

Warm thanks to Mariel Hemingway for touching our family's heart with your loving, truthful, and encouraging words that validate our stories and the power of sharing them.

Huge hugs to Trevor Thompson for understanding that mental health needs to be talked about in a way that brings understanding. This book would not have happened without you!

The support from the community has been overwhelming. Others have made our growth possible: The Meijer Foundation, The Dan and Pamella DeVos Foundation, Celebration Cinema, Biggby Coffee, Mosaic Counseling, Ronald McDonald House of Western Michigan, and countless others. Our partners, followers, and friends mean the world to me. Thank you!

Doug Meijer, i understand would not have become what it is without you! Not only has Doug financially supported i understand; he has created new opportunities for the organization to reach more and more people. When Doug shows up, he always has a smile, words of wisdom to share, a helping hand, and great ideas, and he always wears something pink to show support of unconditional love to all.

I often say to Doug, "Without you, there would be no i understand." He always replies, "Without you, there would be no i understand. I can't do what you do." I respond, "Then it should be 'we understand.'" The greatest gifts I have received were those of unconditional love. I say over and over, "Time doesn't heal. Love heals and can come from the most unexpected places."

There are so many more to thank as I am grateful to all who have touched my heart or broken my heart, believed in me or didn't believe in me. You all have brought me love and pain, yet each has impacted me and brought me to where I am today. Today is a good day.